SOLIDS, LIQUIDS, and GASES

A School Assembly Program
Presenter's Guide

Grades 3–6

Skills
Observing, Comparing, Predicting,
Visualizing, Relating, Modeling

Concepts
Solid, Liquid, Gas, Matter, Energy, Phase, Phase Change,
Evaporation, Sublimation, Condensation, Atom

Themes
Systems & Interactions, Models & Simulations,
Stability, Patterns of Change, Scale,
Structure, Energy, Matter

Nature of Science and Mathematics
Interdisciplinary, Cooperative Efforts, Creativity & Constraints,
Theory-Based and Testable, Real-Life Applications

Jacqueline Barber

LHS GEMS

Great Explorations in Math and Science (GEMS)
Lawrence Hall of Science
University of California, Berkeley

Cover Design
Patricia Flory

Illustrations
Rose Craig
Lisa Klofkorn
Carol Bevilacqua

Photographs
Jacqueline Barber
Marion Buegler
Jim Chapman
Saxon Donnelly
Karen Preuss
Cary Sneider

Lawrence Hall of Science, University of California, Berkeley, CA 94720. Chairman: Glenn T. Seaborg; Director: Marian C. Diamond

Publication was made possible by grants from the A.W. Mellon Foundation and the Carnegie Corporation of New York. This support does not imply responsibility for statements or views expressed in publications of the GEMS program. GEMS also gratefully acknowledges the contribution of word processing equipment from Apple Computer, Inc. Under a grant from the National Science Foundation, GEMS Leader's Workshops have been held across the country. For further information on GEMS leadership opportunities, please contact GEMS at the address and phone number below.

©1986 by The Regents of the University of California. All rights reserved. Printed in the United States of America. Reprinted 1992, 1995, 1999.

International Standard Book Number: 0-912511-69-9

COMMENTS WELCOME

Great Explorations in Math and Science (GEMS) is an ongoing curriculum development project. GEMS guides are revised periodically, to incorporate teacher comments and new approaches. We welcome your criticisms, suggestions, helpful hints, and any anecdotes about your experience presenting GEMS activities. Your suggestions will be reviewed each time a GEMS guide is revised. Please send your comments to: GEMS Revisions, c/o Lawrence Hall of Science, University of California, Berkeley, CA 94720. The phone number is (510) 642-7771.

Great Explorations in Math and Science (GEMS) Program

The Lawrence Hall of Science (LHS) is a public science center on the University of California at Berkeley campus. LHS offers a full program of activities for the public, including workshops and classes, exhibits, films, lectures, and special events. LHS is also a center for teacher education and curriculum research and development.

Over the years, LHS staff have developed a multitude of activities, assembly programs, classes, and interactive exhibits. These programs have proven to be successful at the Hall and should be useful to schools, other science centers, museums, and community groups. A number of these guided-discovery activities have been published under the Great Explorations in Math and Science (GEMS) title, after an extensive refinement process that includes classroom testing of trial versions, modifications to ensure the use of easy-to-obtain materials, and carefully written and edited step-by-step instructions and background information to allow presentation by teachers without special background in mathematics or science.

Staff
Glenn T. Seaborg, Principal Investigator
Jacqueline Barber, Director
Cary Sneider, Curriculum Specialist
Katharine Barrett, John Erickson, Jaine Kopp, Kimi Hosoume, Laura Lowell, Linda Lipner, Carolyn Willard, Staff Development Specialists
Jan M. Goodman, Mathematics Consultant
Cynthia Ashley, Administrative Coordinator
Gabriela Solomon, Distribution Coordinator
Lisa Haderlie Baker, Art Director
Carol Bevilacqua and Lisa Klofkorn, Designers
Lincoln Bergman and Kay Fairwell, Editors

Contributing Authors
Leigh Agler
Jeremy Ahouse
Jacqueline Barber
Katharine Barrett
Lincoln Bergman
Marion E. Buegler
David Buller
Linda De Lucchi
Jean Echols
Alan Gould
Cheryll Hawthorne
Sue Jagoda
Jefferey Kaufmann
Robert C. Knott
Larry Malone
Cary I. Sneider
Elizabeth Stage
Jennifer Meux White

Reviewers

We would like to thank the following educators who reviewed, tested, or coordinated the reviewing of GEMS assembly program and exhibit materials in manuscript form. Their critical comments and recommendations contributed significantly to these GEMS publications. Their participation does not necessarily imply endorsement of the GEMS program.

FINLAND
Sture Björk
Åbo Akademi, Vasa

KENTUCKY
Amy S. Lowen
Theresa H. Mattei
Mike Plamp
Dr. William M. Sudduth
Museum of History and Science, Louisville
Ken Rosenbaum
Jefferson County Public Schools, Louisville

NEW YORK
Sigrin Newell
Discovery Center, Albany

NORTH CAROLINA
Jorge Escobar
James D. Keighton
Paul Nicholson
North Carolina Museum of Life and Science, Durham
Ed Gray
Sue Griswold
Mike Jordan
John Paschal
Cathy Preiss
Carol Sawyer
Patricia J. Wainland
Discovery Place, Charlotte

OREGON
Shab Levy
Oregon Museum of Science and Industry

WASHINGTON
David Foss
Stuart Kendall
Dennis Schatz
William C. Schmitt
David Taylor
Pacific Science Center, Seattle

Contents

Acknowledgments	viii
Introduction	1
Sample Script	3
1. Chemists Experiment	3
A. What Do Chemists Do?	3
B. Giant Test-Tube Experiment	4
2. Define Matter/Energy: Quiz	5
3. Classify Solids, Liquids, and Gases	7
A. Classification Game	7
B. Slides	8
4. Investigate Phase Changes	10
A. Strawberry Gas: Fast Evaporators	11
B. Dry Ice: Sublimation	12
C. Iodine Gas: Sublimation	14
D. On Other Planets	15
5. Introduce the Concept of Atoms	16
A. What Is Matter Made Of?	16
B. How Many Atoms Are in My Body?	16
C. Atoms Are Always Moving	17
6. Model Arrangements of Atoms in Solids, Liquids, and Gases	17
A. Dot Model/BB Model	17
B. People Model	18
7. Applying the Concepts	19
A. Balloon in Liquid Nitrogen	19
B. Parsley in Liquid Nitrogen	20
C. Nitinol Wire	21
8. Conclusion	21

Program Outline	22
Presenting the Assembly Program	25
Demonstrations and Materials	30
1. Giant Test-Tube Experiment	31
2. Matter/Energy Quiz	33
3. Classification Game	34
4. Strawberry Gas	35
5. Dry Ice	36
6. Iodine Gas	37
7. How Many Atoms Are In My Body?	38
8. Atoms Are Always Moving	38
9. Dot Model/BB Model	39
10. & 11. Balloon and Parsley in Liquid Nitrogen	40
12. Nitinol Wire	42
13. Light Box	44
14. Spotlight on a Light Stand	45
15. Overhead Projector	46
16. Slide Projector and Slides	47
17. Power Strip and Extension Cords	48
18. Microphone	48
Checklist of Materials	49
Setting Up at the Site	53
List of Slides	55
Checklist of Last-Minute Tasks	56
Literature Connections	57

Acknowledgments

Solids, Liquids, and Gases was developed by Jacqueline Barber with assistance from Larry Look, Jefferey Kaufmann, and Dan Benoit. Each assembly presenter has left an original imprint on the program, adapting it to suit particular audiences and locales, and many of these contributions have been incorporated into this sample script. The final version was written by Jacqueline Barber with invaluable assistance from Larry Malone. A special thanks to the Principal Investigator of the GEMS Program, Dr. Glenn T. Seaborg, for corrections in this second edition, relating to the periodic table charts on page 15, and for the same corrections in the slide package that can also be ordered for this program.

Introduction

Picture an auditorium filled with elementary school students, their attention riveted on a large balloon atop an enormous test tube. The students are asked to predict what will happen when a solid and liquid are mixed in the test tube. Then they applaud with delight when their predictions come true—the mixture in the test tube fizzes and bubbles, and the balloon is inflated with gas.

The *Solids, Liquids, and Gases* assembly program can add a dynamic dimension to your science center's link with the public, whether the program is presented at your institution or packed into a van for presentation at schools and community centers. This form of community outreach is an economically viable way of increasing the impact of limited personnel and resources, as well as enhancing school science curricula in new and exciting ways. This assembly program gives an instructor exciting demonstrations and audience participation techniques that actively involve people in learning about science.

In this program, the audience attempts to predict the results of a number of experiments, sometimes with surprising or unexpected results: a flask glows with violet gas, parsley shatters when it is crushed, a red liquid turns into strawberry-scented gas. By the time the students leave the *Solids, Liquids, and Gases* assembly program, they are excited about science, and have a better understanding of the properties of matter and how it can change from one phase to another.

Solids, Liquids and Gases can be used to kick off a classroom unit on matter, phase change, or a more extensive unit on chemistry. If used as a single encounter, this program can spark student interest in science and science-related careers.

Like a theater production that requires a substantial investment of time and materials, an assembly program should be planned for numerous audiences and presentations. While this planning could be accomplished by an individual, the support and wide audience of a school district or science center is desirable.

This guide includes a script and descriptions of the experiments. Do not memorize the script, instead use it as a guide in developing your own program. A one-page outline is provided as a cue-sheet to be used during the presentation. Next is a section with suggestions for transporting and setting up materials, and hints on large-group presentation techniques. As you read the script, you will see references to demonstrations and materials. These are fully explained later in the guide.

The script is intended for students in grades three through six, but can be adapted for kindergarteners, high school students, or adults. You will need to adjust the length and timing of the program each time you present it, due to differences in audience response. The program can also incorporate other experiments and concepts that are appropriate to different audiences. Use the guide to **expand** your ideas, not limit them!

Sample Script: Solids, Liquids, and Gases

1. Chemists Experiment

A. What Do Chemists Do?

Hello everybody, I'm happy to be here at the _____ School to present *Solids, Liquids, and Gases*. I've brought lots of chemistry equipment with me today so we can do some experiments.

For thousands of years, people have been doing chemistry experiments. That's another way of saying that people have been trying to find out more about what things are made of, and what happens when you mix different materials together and why. The first time people were employed as chemists was about 300 years ago; they were known as **alchemists**. [Slide #1: picture of an alchemist.] Alchemists worked hard to turn ordinary metal into gold. Raise your hand if you think they were successful. [Pause for response.] Although they weren't successful at producing gold, they did figure out a lot about what things are made of.

Chemists are still experimenting to find out about the world. [Slides #2 and #3: modern day chemist and students doing chemistry.] Though chemists have discovered many things, much of what's in the universe remains a mystery. There are still many experiments that need to be done, and we're going to do some of them today. But first, I need to put on my lab coat, not to *look* like a scientist but, more importantly, to *protect* me in the event of a spill. [Put on lab coat at this point.] I also have my safety goggles and gloves here, ready for me when I need them.

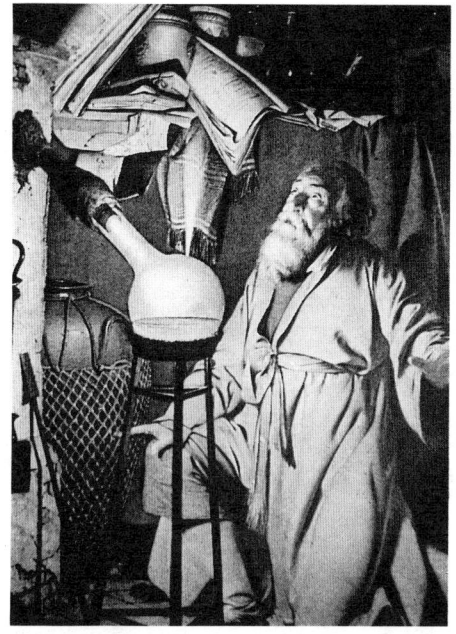

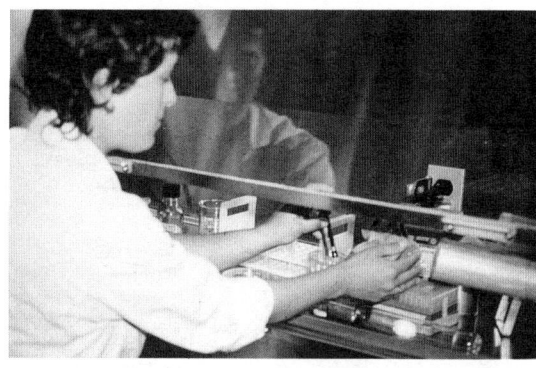

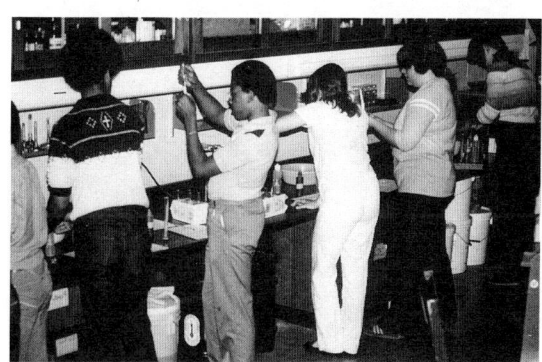

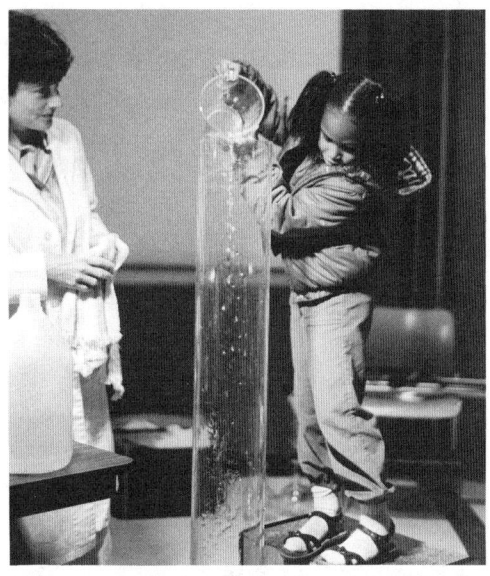

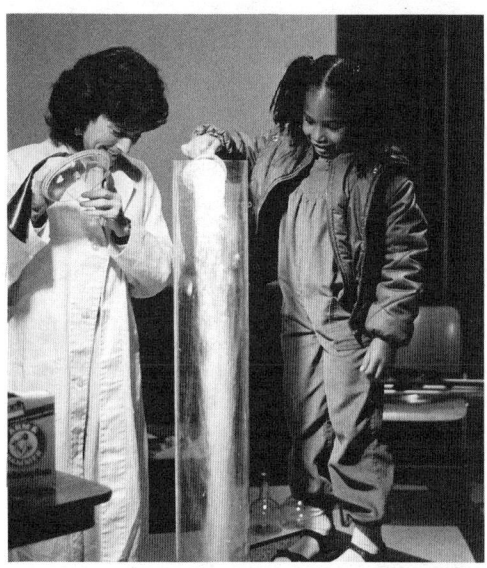

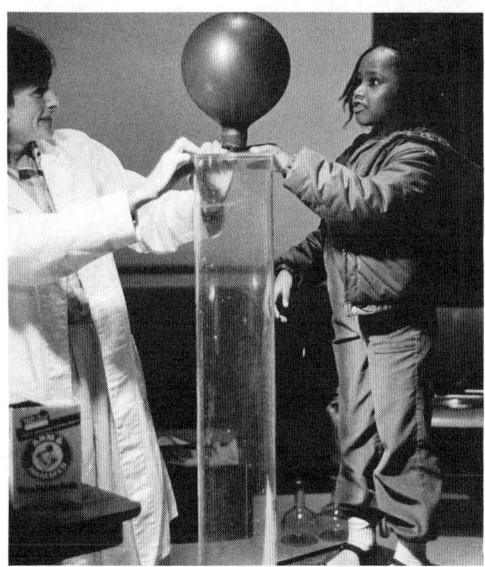

B. Giant Test-Tube Experiment

Let's do an experiment and see what we can discover. I need two volunteers. [Select two volunteers.] I brought a *small* test tube, so we can do just a *small* experiment. [Show giant test tube.] I'd like you [to one of the volunteers] to help by pouring a *liquid* into the test tube. [On light box, pour one quart of vinegar into the four-cup measure. Say to the volunteer:] Tell the audience what liquid we have here. [Wait for response.] Vinegar! It's the same kind of vinegar that we eat on our salads. [Have volunteer pour vinegar into the giant tube.]

Now let's have our other volunteer add a *solid* to this *liquid*. [On the light box, pour baking soda into the one-cup measure. Say to the audience:] The solid we are going to add to the vinegar is called *baking soda,* the same kind used in baking cakes. Some of you chemists may have already done this experiment.

Raise your hand if you can predict what might happen when we add the baking soda to the vinegar. [Call on several students.] Just for fun, I'm going to put this lid on top of the tube, after she adds the baking soda. [Show the lid.] There's a hole in the lid. [To audience:] What's attached to the hole? [A balloon. Say to the volunteer:] Okay, on the count of three, you pour the baking soda into the tube. [To audience:] Let's all count. One.... two.... three!!! [Volunteer dumps in baking soda, you attach the lid, hold it with both hands, and everyone watches the balloon inflate.]

We added a *solid* to a *liquid* and made what? Raise your hand. [A *gas*.] We can't tell by just looking what kind of *gas* we made, but raise your hand if you would like to guess. [Call on several students.] Raise your hand if you've heard of *carbon dioxide* gas. We just made carbon dioxide gas by mixing baking soda and vinegar. There are lots of ways to make carbon dioxide gas. Everyone breathe out. Your bodies just made carbon dioxide gas. Part of what we breathe out is carbon dioxide gas. Let's have a hand for our volunteers. [Have the volunteers return to their seats.]

2. Define Matter/Energy: Quiz

Of course, chemists experiment with a lot more than just baking soda and vinegar. Chemists experiment with *matter*. This isn't the same kind of matter as in "What's the matter?" or "Does this matter to you?". Chemists define *matter* as anything that takes up space. [Repeat.] *Matter is anything in the universe that has mass (or weight) and takes up space.*

Let's have a little quiz. [Knock on the table.] Does this table take up space? Does it have mass (or weight)? Is this table made of matter? Yes.

How about me, are people made of matter? [Touch yourself.] Yes, I have mass and occupy space.

Okay, let's make this a little harder. [Wave your hands through the air.] Air... Raise your hand if you think air has mass and takes up space—if you think air is matter. Now raise your hand to show if you think, "no way—air is not matter." Now watch what I do. [Pick up a balloon, fill it with air, and tie it.] Now let's have another vote: raise your hand if you think air is not matter. Let me offer some more evidence to those of you who aren't convinced that air *does* take up space. The air in this balloon takes up the entire space inside the balloon. If I make the space smaller... [squeeze the balloon—POP!!!]... the air has no place to go, so it bursts out the sides of the balloon. *Even though you can't see it, air takes up space; even though you can't always feel it, air has weight.* So air is matter!

Now watch closely... [if you have an assistant, wave your hand for the house lights to go on and off, or, if not, switch light box lamp on and off a couple of times.] Raise your hand if you think light is matter... has mass and takes up space. Now raise your hand if you think light is something *besides* matter. Light does not have mass, nor does it take up space; light is energy. Everything in the universe that we know about is either *matter* or *energy*. Light is one example of energy.

[Hold hand over hot plate.] This hot plate is giving out a lot of heat. Some of you in the front rows might be able to feel the heat coming from here. Raise your hand if you think heat is energy. This is a tough one for me to prove to you, so I'll tell you. ***Heat is energy.***

Now this is a tricky one... watch closely. [Ignite flash paper by touching it to the hot plate.] Fire... Raise your hand if you think fire is matter. Now raise your hand if you think fire is energy. Watch again. This time, see if you can see where the fire goes. [Ignite flash paper again.] Raise your hand if you can smell a burning odor. An odor lets us know that there is a gas present. When that paper burned, it left behind some gases—and gases are matter. Part of fire is matter. However, part of fire is not matter—it is light and heat. Light and heat are two examples of energy. So if you raised your hand when I asked if fire was matter, you were right. If you raised your hand when I asked if fire was energy, you were right too! Everybody was right because fire is both matter and energy at the same time.

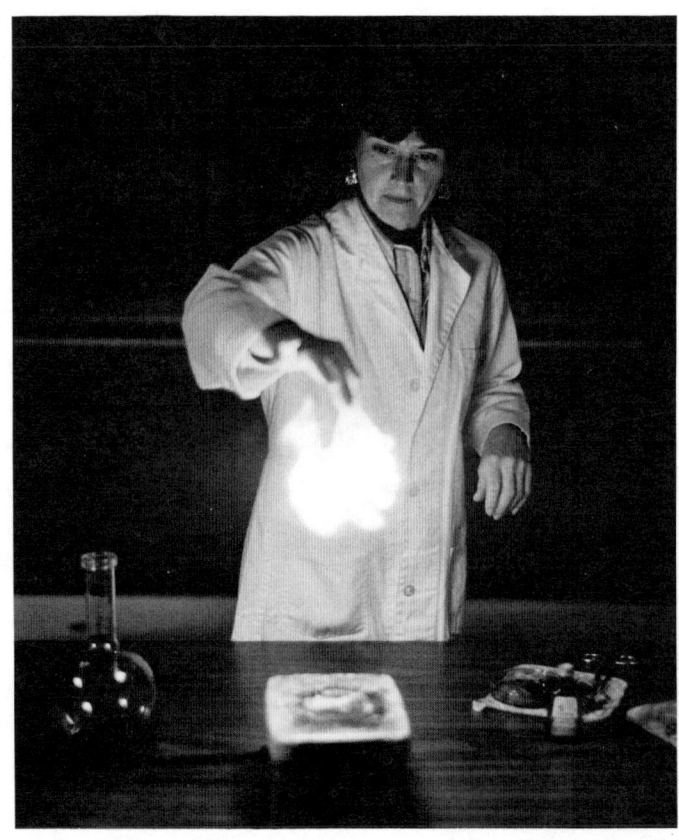

3. Classify Solids, Liquids, and Gases

A. Classification Game

When we did the experiment in the giant test tube, we added a solid to a liquid and made what? [Gas.] Chemists have discovered that all matter can exist in either a *solid phase*, a *liquid phase*, or a *gas phase*.

I need three volunteers. [Hand each of the three volunteers a necklace sign that reads "SOLID," "LIQUID," or "GAS".] These volunteers are each going to be in charge of one of the phases of matter: solid, liquid, or gas. [To audience:] Your job will be to let me know to whom I should give each object.

Let's start out with something easy. [Hold up a rock.] Who should I give this rock to? This is an easy one. Does it spill? Can I put my finger through it? Does it float away? . . . three easy tests for a solid. [Hand the rock to the volunteer with the "SOLID" sign.]

Now that you've got the hang of it, let's try something a little more difficult. [Take the large balloon full of carbon dioxide gas from the giant tube experiment. Remove it from the lid carefully to keep the gas in it, and hold it up.] Who should I give this to? [Turn to the volunteer with the "GAS" sign. Ask him to hold out his hand. Empty the gas from the balloon into his hand. The audience often laughs here; wait for the laughter to subside.] Was it fair to ask him to hold on to a gas? Gases escape. They're difficult to contain. For him to have held on to a gas, I would have needed to give him a balloon or some other closed container. That was an unfair request. Now the carbon dioxide we made is loose in the room. That's what happens when there's a gas leak from your stove or heater; the gas escapes into the room.

Okay, so there was a gas in this balloon, but what's the balloon made of? Raise your hand if you think this rubber balloon is a solid. Raise your hand if you think it's a liquid. Let's do our tests: Does it spill? Can I put my finger through it? Will an empty balloon float away? Three easy tests for a what? [Wait for responses.] A solid! So this rubber balloon is a solid. [Give the balloon to the volunteer with the "SOLID" sign.]

B. Slides

[Show Slide #4: hot air balloon.] By containing certain gases, you can get them to work for you. The gas in this balloon is being used for transportation. Raise your hand if you know what gas it might be. [Call on several students.] The important thing about this gas is that it's lighter than air; it enables the balloon to float up in the sky. The gas in this balloon is hot air. Hydrogen gas and helium gas are also lighter than air.

[Hold up a flask of water, swirling the liquid in it.] Solid, liquid, or gas? Water is the most common liquid on earth. [Threaten to pour water into the outstretched hand of the "LIQUID" volunteer, then stop short.] Raise your hand if you think the glass container is a solid. Raise your hand if you think it's a liquid. [Go through the tests for a solid on the flask.] Though glass *seems* to pass the tests for a solid, it turns out that glass is a liquid. Glass flows. Right now, the glass in this flask is flowing very slowly. Evidence to support the fact that glass is a liquid can be seen on old windows. Raise your hand if you've seen a very old window. Sometimes you can see something that looks like oozing on glass that is 50 years old or more. If we were to measure the thickness of an old window at both the top and bottom, we'd find that it is thicker at the bottom. That's because gravity is causing the glass to flow down. [Show Slide #5 of old glass bottle.] If you look at this old bottle, you can see how the glass is flowing downward. Glass is a tricky one to classify because it seems to have properties of both solids and liquids. Liquids flow. Glass flows. Glass is a liquid.

[Hold a flower, a piece of fruit, or a vegetable as you ask the following questions.]

- Raise your hand if you think this banana contains solid.

- Raise your hand if you think we could squeeze some liquid out of it.

- Raise your hand if you think it was once alive.

- Raise your hand if you think living things need gases to stay alive.

- What gases do plants use? [Carbon dioxide, oxygen.]

- Raise your hand if you think there might still be some gas in the cells of this banana.

- Raise your hand if you think this banana is solid, liquid, *and* gas.

It's not just bananas that have solids, liquids, and gases in them. Anything that's alive or very recently alive, like this banana—all plants and animals—have solids, liquids, and gases in them. So who should I give the banana to? This game is going to get harder and harder to play, because most things in the world are some combination of solids, liquids, and gases. Our volunteers would be trying to pull apart everything I brought out!

[Show Slide #6: ginger ale.] Raise your hand to say what you think is in ginger ale. [Call on several students.] Inside those bubbles are gas. Ginger ale is liquid and gas. [Show Slide #7: milk.] Though milk seems like a liquid it actually has many tiny solids suspended all through it. If you were to dissolve some chocolate powder in milk to make chocolate milk, you'd have even more solid in it.

Let's have a hand for our volunteers. They were good sports. [Have the volunteers return to their seats.]

4. Investigate Phase Changes

How could you change ice—a solid—to water—a liquid? Raise your hand if you have an idea. [Heat it.] What did we say heat was? [Energy.] ***By adding energy to a solid, you can change it to a liquid.*** How could you change water from a liquid to a gas? [Heat it more.] And what did we say heat was? [Energy.] ***By adding energy to a liquid, you can change it to a gas.*** Adding and subtracting energy allows you to change matter from phase to phase. Let's experiment by adding energy to matter and seeing what happens.

A. Strawberry Gas: Fast Evaporators

I have a liquid here. [Turn overhead projector on. Pour strawberry extract into glass Petri dish on projector.] How could we turn this liquid into a gas? Raise your hand if you have an idea. What did we say heat was? [Energy.] We can put this dish on the hot plate.

Before we do, I have a couple of questions. What is it called when something changes from liquid to gas phase? *[Evaporation.]* How will we know if this liquid is evaporating? [See steam, less liquid, boiling.]

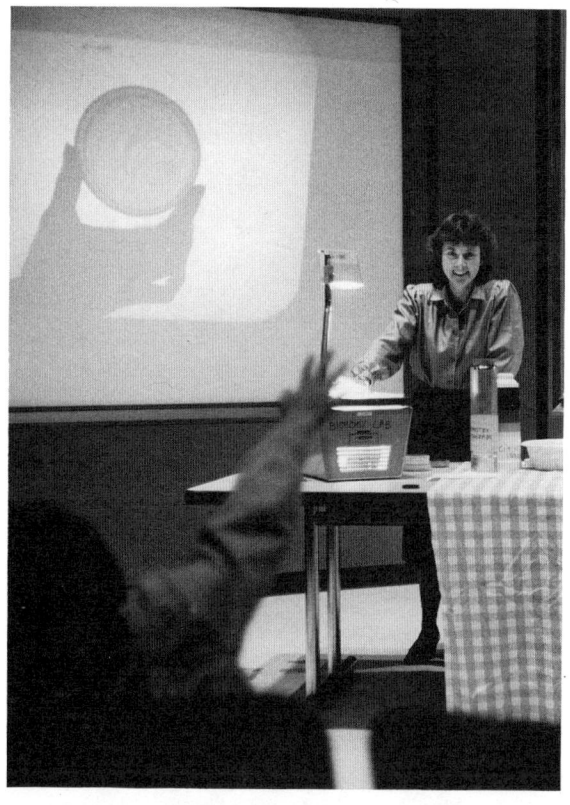

What I didn't tell you about this liquid is that it smells like strawberries. Raise your hand if you smell strawberries. Small amounts of the strawberry liquid have evaporated from this dish, gone into the air, and are floating out in the audience and into your noses. Energy from the room and the hot plate has caused the liquid to start evaporating—changing to a gas. The evidence that strawberry gas is present is that we can smell it. *Remember: if you can smell it, it's a gas.* However, bear in mind that *not all* gases have odors. Air and water vapor are examples of gases we can't smell.

Let's experiment by adding *more* energy to the strawberry liquid and see what happens. When I put the liquid on the hot plate, the heat energy will speed up evaporation. If you smell strawberry gas, raise your hand and keep it up. Let's all watch and see how the strawberry gas travels in the room. Before we start, discuss with your neighbor which direction the gas will travel in the room. [Wait 15 seconds.] Here we go. [Put the liquid on the hot plate. After a minute or so, have the audience lower their hands and ask those who don't smell the

Sample Script **11**

strawberry gas to raise their hands. Let the experiment continue for two or three minutes, then instruct everyone to put their hands down.] Point to the direction the strawberry gas traveled. Raise your hand if you have an explanation. [The windows are open; the ventilation or heating systems are circulating the air, etc.]

Raise your hand if you've ever smelled a rock. Raise your hand if you think we'd smell a rock more if we added energy—heated it up. Certain substances are fast evaporators, like this strawberry liquid or perfume. It takes just a little energy to change them to gases. Rocks, on the other hand, are very stubborn. You have to add many thousands of degrees to change a rock to a liquid—to lava. And it takes much more heat to change liquid rock to a gas. Raise your hand if you ever brought a banana to school in your lunch box. Raise your hand if you smelled banana when you opened your lunch box. That odor meant that some of your banana changed to a gas. If you can smell it, it's a gas. The things that give off the most odor are the fastest evaporators.

B. Dry Ice: Sublimation

Raise your hands if you've ever seen dry ice. I brought some dry ice today. Dry ice is made of frozen carbon dioxide gas. Carbon dioxide gas becomes a solid when it is cooled down to 110 degrees below zero (Fahrenheit). [Put on a glove.] It is so cold that I need to protect my skin by wearing this glove. [Take out a piece of dry ice. Hit it on the surface of the light box so kids can hear that it is a solid. Ask the following questions, calling on several students for their ideas after each question.]

- What do you see happening to the dry ice as I hold it here? Is it melting or evaporating?

- It is changing to a gas. What ideas do you have for why it is changing to a gas now? [It's getting heat from the lamp.]

- And what did we say heat was? [Energy.]

- By adding energy to this dry ice we're changing it from a solid to what? A gas!

This is a special case. If we were to heat regular ice, it would turn to liquid first, and then to a gas. Dry ice is called dry ice because it goes straight from the solid phase to the gas phase. When liquid changes to gas, it's called what? [Evaporation.] When a solid changes directly to a gas, it's called *sublimation*. This dry ice is *subliming.* Remember the word *subliming,* because I'm going to ask you about it later.

How could we get this dry ice to sublime faster? Raise your hand. [By putting the dry ice on the hot plate.] We could add more heat—more energy. I have some hot water. Let's put the dry ice in the hot water and see what happens. [Pour warm water from the kettle into a clear container that has a few drops of food coloring (blue or green) in the bottom. Put the dry ice in the water. Your audience will be excited because of the eerie vapor. After 30 seconds or so, blow across the top of the container... more oohs and ahhs.] Raise your hand if you've seen a scary movie that has "fog" like this blowing across the scene. Now you know how they create this special effect: they take dry ice, or something very cold, add energy to it, and have a fan operating behind it.

Is carbon dioxide gas visible? Let's do a small experiment to find out. Everyone breathe out. Could you see the carbon dioxide you exhaled? No. Carbon dioxide gas is invisible. Raise your hand if you've been to a very cold place during the winter and seen something that looks like this "fog" when you breathe out. What you're seeing is the *water vapor* in the air you exhale, turning back to a liquid. Air, especially the air we breathe out, is full of water in a gas phase—water vapor. When the air gets very cold, the evaporated water turns back to a liquid; it *condenses.* That is what is happening here. Lots of cold carbon dioxide gas is pouring out of this container, too. We can't see either of these two invisible gases. What we're seeing is condensed water vapor—tiny droplets of liquid water suspended in the air like fog or a cloud.

Teachers of middle school students may be interested in a new GEMS teacher's guide for Grades 6–8 entitled Dry Ice Investigations. *In addition to providing students with much information on phase change and sublimation, the unit places special emphasis on making use of the captivating properties of dry ice to improve student understandings of and ability to engage in scientific inquiry.*

C. Iodine Gas: Sublimation

[While the audience is still focused on the dry ice, set the Florence flask on the hot plate.] Let's do another experiment. Take a look at the screen. [Turn on the overhead projector. Shake 4–6 small iodine crystals into a Petri dish.] Raise your hand if you can see some small, black crystals. These are iodine crystals. What do you predict will happen if we add energy to these iodine crystals? Raise your hand. [They might melt, disappear, etc.] Let's try it. I've heated this flask. We'll add energy by putting the crystals in the hot flask. [Remove the heated flask from the hot plate. Place it on top of a piece of screen on the light box. The screen protects the wood surface of the light box. Empty the Petri dish with iodine crystals into the hot flask. **Quickly stopper the flask, because iodine gas is toxic.**] Raise your hand if you see violet gas. What is it called when a solid changes directly to a gas? [Sublimation.] The iodine crystals sublimed. Iodine gas is one of the few visible gases. Most gases are invisible. I put the stopper in the flask because it is dangerous to breathe iodine gas. What do you think will happen as this flask cools off—as it loses energy? Raise your hand. Remind me at the end of the program to take a look at the flask. It will be fairly cool by then.

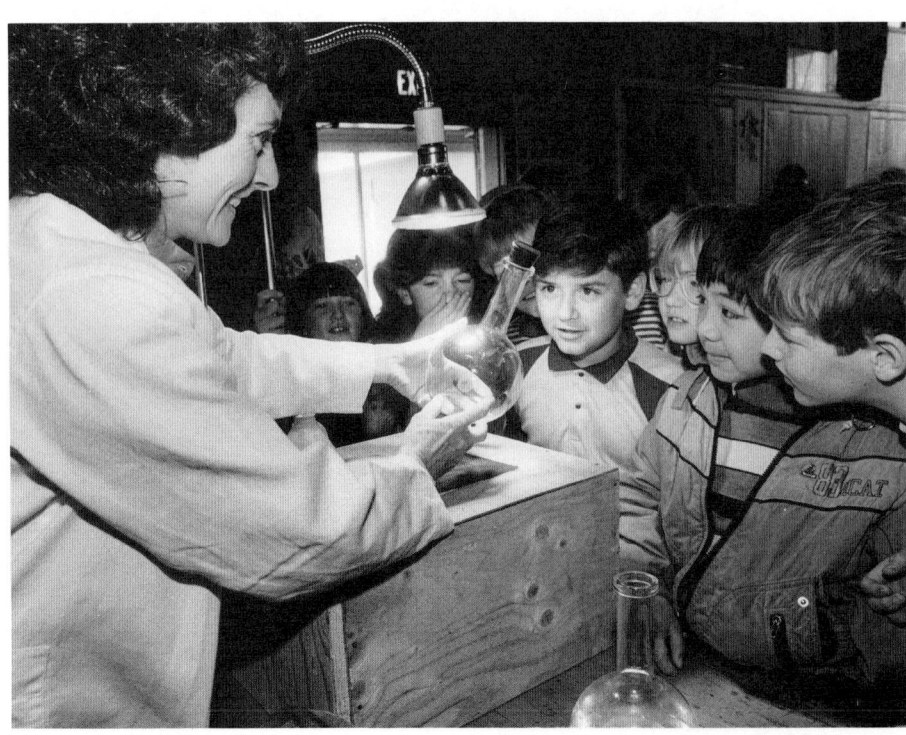

D. On Other Planets

If we were to gather all of the various substances on the Earth, we would find that, at 60 degrees Fahrenheit, most of them are solids. There would be some gases and only a few liquids [Show Slide #8: elements at 60 degrees Fahrenheit (15.5 degrees Celsius), color coded by phase.] What would happen if we were to lower the temperature dramatically? Imagine that we could take all the elements from Earth much farther away from the sun, where it is much colder, to the planet Pluto. On Pluto the average noon temperature is about −346 degrees Fahrenheit, or −210 degrees Celsius. Raise your hand if you think we could expect to find the same number of solids, liquids, and gases at that low temperature. [Show Slide #9: elements at −346 degrees Fahrenheit, color coded by phase.] If we were able to bring all of these elements to the cold temperature of Pluto, we would find that there would be even more solids than on Earth; almost everything would be in the solid phase. On the other hand, what if we were able to transport these substances much closer to the sun, to the planet Mercury? The average noon temperature on Mercury is about 788 degrees Fahrenheit, or 420 degrees Celsius. How might this big increase in temperature affect the phases of matter? Raise your hand. [Show Slide #10: elements at 788 degrees Fahrenheit, color coded by phase.] In the heat on the planet Mercury, we would find that many substances were gases and liquids. There would be more liquids than at the 60 degree Fahrenheit temperature on Earth.

Chemists have discovered that by continuing to heat things hotter and hotter, until they reach over 11,000 degrees Fahrenheit or 6,128 degrees Celsius, all things become gases: metal, concrete, and even people. If one adds enough energy, all matter will be vaporized into gas! And, if you take enough energy away, if you cool things down to −460 degrees Fahrenheit (−273 degrees Celsius), everything in the universe will freeze solid except possibly one substance—helium. Helium gas will change to a liquid, but scientists have not yet been able to make solid helium.

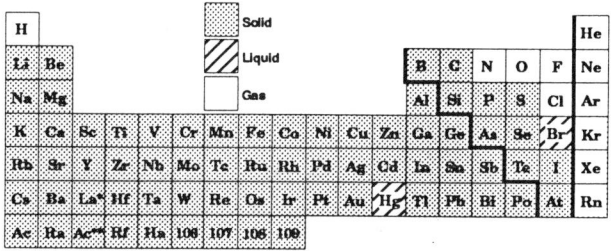

Periodic Table of the Elements on the Planet Earth
(60° Fahrenheit)

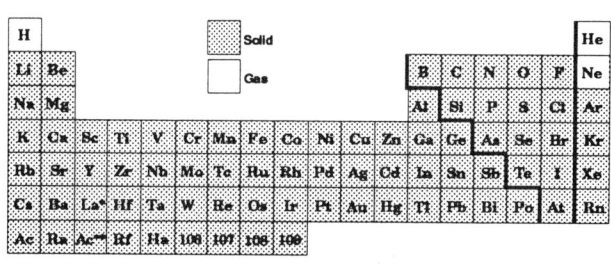

Periodic Table of the Elements on the Planet Pluto
(-346° Fahrenheit)

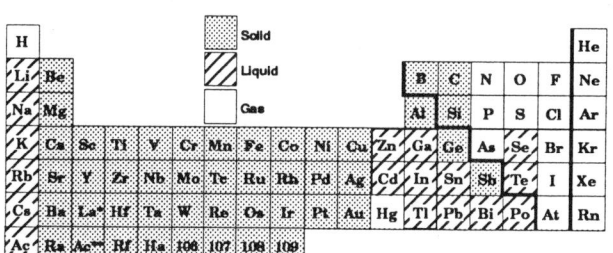

Periodic Table of the Elements on the Planet Mercury
(788° Fahrenheit)

Note: In 1997, element 106 officially became seaborgium (Sg), after Nobel Laureate Glenn T. Seaborg, co-discoverer of plutonium and many transuranium elements. Dr. Seaborg was Principal Investigator of the GEMS Program.

5. Introduce the Concept of *Atoms*

A. What Is Matter Made Of?

We talked earlier about how solids, liquids, and gases are all matter. What do you think matter is made of that allows it to be dense sometimes and flow or float at other times? Raise your hand if you have an idea about what matter is made of. [Common answers are: gas, carbon dioxide, molecules, space, atoms.] Raise your hand if you've heard of atoms. Matter is made of atoms; all solids, liquids, and gases are made of atoms.

B. How Many Atoms Are in My Body?

[Hold up a standard yellow pencil.] Is this how big an atom is? How about just the eraser? Is that how big an atom is? *Atoms are so small that there's no way they can be seen with the naked eye.* In fact, scientists have only recently developed microscopes powerful enough to see the largest atoms.

I am made of matter, so I must be made of atoms. Let's figure out how many. If I took the eraser off this pencil, along with a *million* more erasers, they would fill a bathtub. A *billion* erasers would fill a house, and a *trillion* erasers would fill 1,000 houses. But I have more than a trillion atoms in my body. If I filled those 1,000 houses full of erasers and dumped them out, and refilled them and dumped them out, and continued to do it a trillion times, I would have erasers up to my armpits over the entire surface of our Earth and 1,000 more planets just like it! But that's still not enough. It would take 10 million planets the size of Earth, all covered five feet deep in erasers, to equal the number of atoms in my body. As you can see, atoms are very small.

So, the first thing to remember about atoms is that they're really tiny.

C. Atoms Are Always Moving

I want you all to pretend that you can see an atom. I'm going to turn out the lights and show you a model of what scientists think atoms might look like. [Turn out lights. Turn on fiber optics wand and move it quickly and constantly, causing strands of fiber optics to fly around the lit center of the wand.] Can you see the lit-up center? That represents the nucleus: the center of the atom. Can you see the little spots of light moving all around the *nucleus?* Those represent the *electrons.* Notice how the atom is moving all around.

The second thing to remember about atoms is that they're always moving.

6. Model Arrangements of Atoms in Solids, Liquids, and Gases

A. Dot Model/BB Model

Keep pretending that you can see atoms, but this time pretend that one atom is one dot. [Turn on the overhead projector. Project the overlay of atoms in a solid on the screen.] See that pile of atoms? This is what chemists think the atoms in a solid would look like. Notice how they're packed together in a regular pattern. But what did we say about atoms? Atoms are always... what? [Moving.] So really, a better model of what the atoms in a solid would look like is this. [Take overlay off overhead. Place the plastic Petri *full of BBs* on the overhead, and gently move the Petri dish back and forth so the BBs are vibrating.]

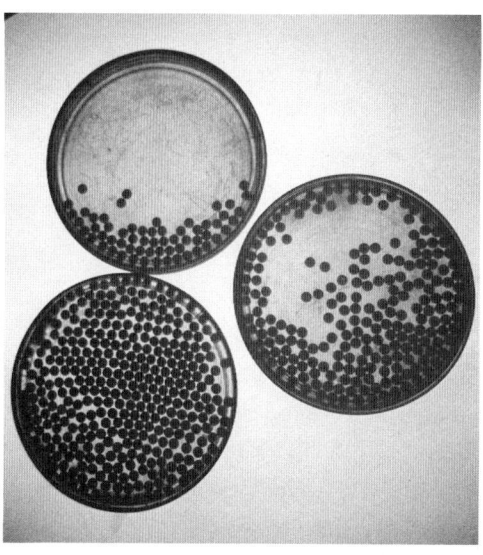

[Remove the BB model from overhead, and project the overlay of atoms in a liquid.] This is what chemists think atoms in a liquid would look like. Notice how they are less organized than the atoms in a solid, and how there is more space between these atoms. But what did we say? Atoms are always... [moving.] So a better model of what the atoms in a liquid would look like is this. [Remove the overlay and place the plastic Petri *half full of BBs* on the overhead, moving the Petri dish back and forth faster than you did with the "solid" BB model.]

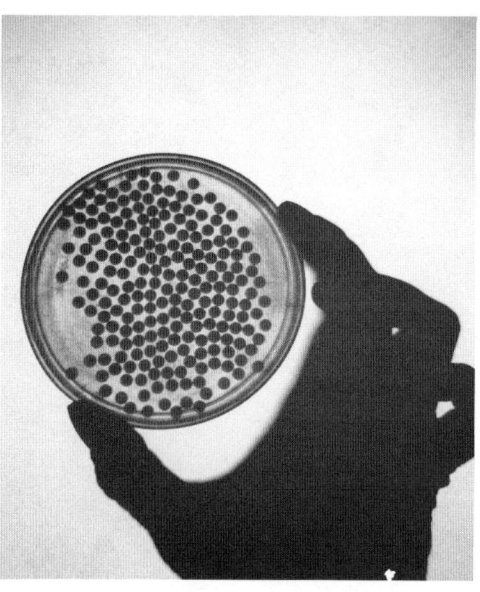

[Remove the BB model from the overhead, and project the overlay of atoms in a gas.] What do you think this represents? [A gas!] See how the atoms are escaping out of the top of the container? However, *we* know that atoms are always moving, so here's a better model. [Remove the overlay and place the plastic Petri with a *half dozen BBs* in it on the overhead. Move the Petri dish rapidly back and forth, so the BBs appear as a blur.

Watch as I change a solid to a gas. [Start with the BB solid model, vibrating the dish slowly. Switch to the BB liquid model, moving faster. End with the BB gas model, moving the dish as fast as you can.] As we add energy, matter goes from the solid phase to the liquid phase to the gas phase. The more energy we add, the more energy these atoms have. By taking energy away (cooling it down), we can change a gas back to liquid, and then back to a solid. [Demonstrate this sequence of a gas changing to a liquid changing to a solid.] The more energy we take away, the less energy the atoms have.

B. People Model

I need some volunteers. [Choose ten volunteers.] These people just volunteered to be atoms. First they're going to have to "be" a solid, then a liquid, and then a gas.

Okay, be a solid. [Volunteers invariably look blankly at each other. Help them out with some coaxing.] Should I be able to get my hand between these two atoms? [To volunteers:] Squish together! Solids are dense, you can't put your finger through them. [Turn to audience:] Atoms are always what? [Moving!] Vibrate, you atoms! Now that's more like it!

Now, be a liquid. [To audience, whether the volunteers are doing it or not:] Notice how they're moving faster, and spreading farther apart! That's good.

Now for a gas... Great! They've spread way out, and they're moving so fast that they're bumping off of one another! Not bad!

18 Sample Script

Okay, that was good, but it was too easy. This time I'm not going to tell them what phase to be in, I'm just going to add energy to the atoms and see what happens. Start out as a solid. Here goes. I'm adding energy... more energy... more... more... I'd say we're nearing maximum energy. Notice how the more energy I add, the more energy they have. Now I'm taking energy away, cooling these atoms down... down... down... until they've reached the solid phase again. Let's have a hand for these atoms. They were excellent! [Have the volunteers return to their seats.]

7. Applying the Concepts

A. Balloon in Liquid Nitrogen

I saved my three favorite experiments for last. Raise your hand if you've heard of nitrogen. Now, everyone breathe in. You just breathed in nitrogen gas! Although we breathe air for the oxygen gas in it, in fact, air is made mostly of nitrogen gas. Today I brought some liquid nitrogen. Raise your hand if you have an idea how you could turn nitrogen gas into liquid nitrogen. In order to make liquid nitrogen, nitrogen gas is *cooled* to *320 degrees* below zero, Fahrenheit. This liquid is so cold that I need to protect my eyes and my skin. [Put on safety goggles and leather gloves.] When I pour the liquid nitrogen into this container, a lot of it will turn to gas because it's so warm in here compared to −320 degrees. See if you can see the liquid as I pour it. [Pour liquid nitrogen from large Dewar into smaller, tabletop Dewar.]

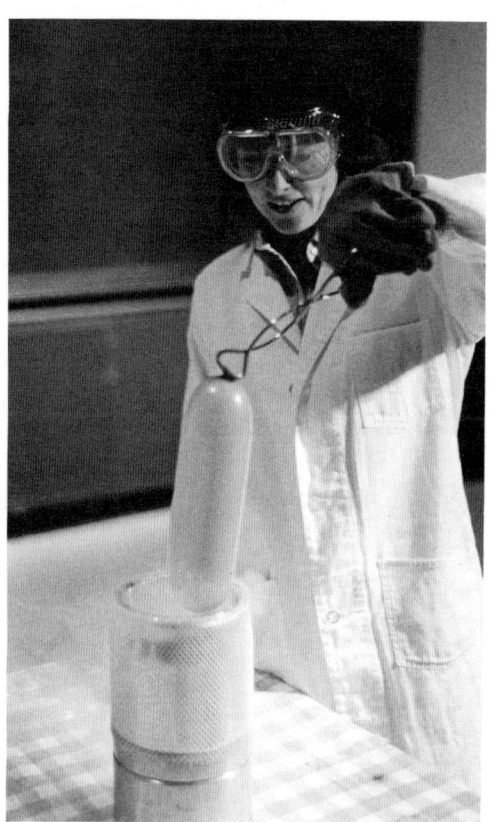

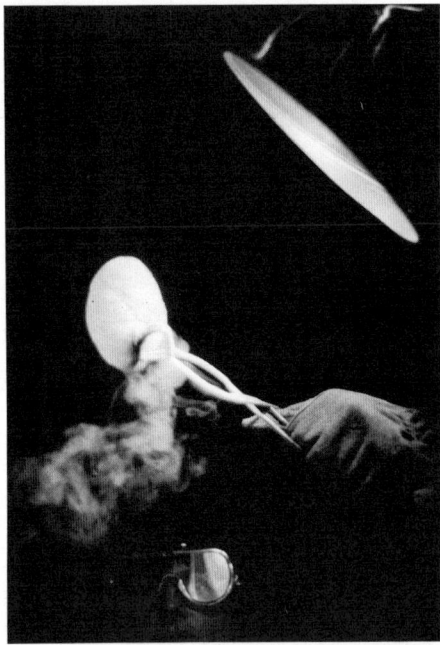

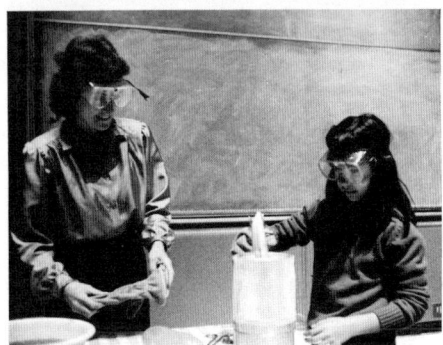

[Hold up an inflated balloon.] Raise your hand if you have a prediction of what might happen when I put this balloon, full of air, into the liquid nitrogen. [Call on several students. Then pick up the balloon with a pair of tongs. Submerge the balloon in liquid nitrogen. Wait several seconds until the nitrogen almost stops boiling. Ask the audience to be absolutely silent. Remove the balloon from the liquid nitrogen and hold it under the spotlight; this works best if you try to heat it evenly with a back-and-forth, rotating motion. The balloon will appear shrunken at first. You may be able to see liquid inside. As the balloon heats up under the light, it will quickly regain its original size and appearance.] Describe what first happened to the balloon. Raise your hand. [It got smaller.] Can anyone explain why the balloon got smaller after it was put in the liquid nitrogen? [When atoms get cold, they move closer together.] **Remember: atoms don't shrink, they move closer together.** Then what happened? Raise your hand. [The balloon got bigger when you put it under the light.] Can anyone explain why it did that? Raise your hand. [As atoms get warmer, they move farther apart.]

B. Parsley in Liquid Nitrogen

[Hold up a bunch of parsley, carrot tops, or other leafy bouquet.] Is parsley a solid, liquid, or gas? Raise your hand. [Solid, liquid, and gas.] Predict what will happen when I put the parsley in the liquid nitrogen. [Hold the parsley with the tongs. Lower the parsley into the liquid nitrogen. Leave it in until the liquid nitrogen almost stops boiling. Ask for the audience's total silence. Remove the parsley from the nitrogen. Hold the parsley under the light. Crush the parsley with your other gloved hand. The parsley will shatter, making the sound of shattered glass.] Who can explain why the parsley shattered? [Call on several students.] All of the liquid and gas in the parsley turned to solid at −320 degrees, Fahrenheit. The parsley turned into a brittle solid that sounds like glass when it shatters.

C. Nitinol Wire

[Turn on the overhead projector. Project a piece of nitinol wire on the screen.] I have some special wire here, called nitinol wire. It is made by mixing nickel and titanium metals. Watch what happens when I try to bend the wire. [Pull back on the top of the wire. It springs back.] We're going to play some temperature games with this piece of wire. I'm going to cool the atoms in this wire way down so they slow down and move closer together. [Pour ice water from the thermos into the plastic dishpan. Submerge the wire. Then wrap it around a pencil. Hold the wire on the overhead projector so the wire's new shape is projected on the screen.] Now what happened when I cooled the wire? [Students will respond: "It stays coiled," "It's like a spring."] Let's put the wire in some warm water. [Put the clock crystal on the overhead projector. Fill the crystal with warm water from the thermos. Hold the wire just over the water's surface so the wire's image is projected on the wall, but so the wire is not touching the water.] I'm holding the wire just over the water. Watch while I slowly put the wire in the hot water. [Lower the wire into the water, a little at a time. The nitinol wire will suddenly straighten.] Who can explain why the wire straightened? Raise your hand. [Call on several students.] [The heat caused the atoms in the wire to move more, and farther apart.]

8. Conclusion

That brings today's presentation to a close, but it really is only a beginning. I hope you enjoyed our scientific investigation of solids, liquids, and gases, and of atoms. This is only a beginning because chemists and other scientists are still doing all kinds of experiments to find out more about what things are made of and what happens when things change, experiments just like those we did today. New discoveries are always being made.

I'd like to thank our volunteers, and to also thank all of you for being such a fine, energetic audience. If you have any questions, in the time remaining I'd be glad to explore them with you.

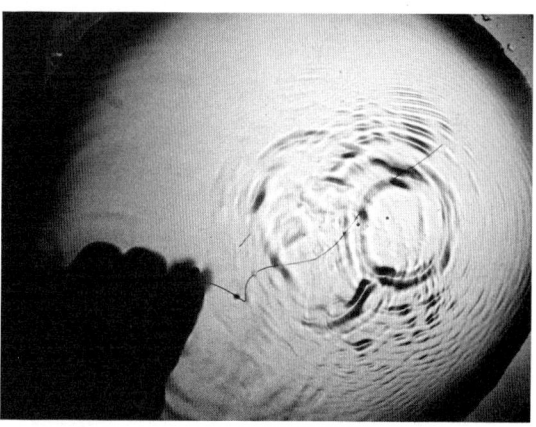
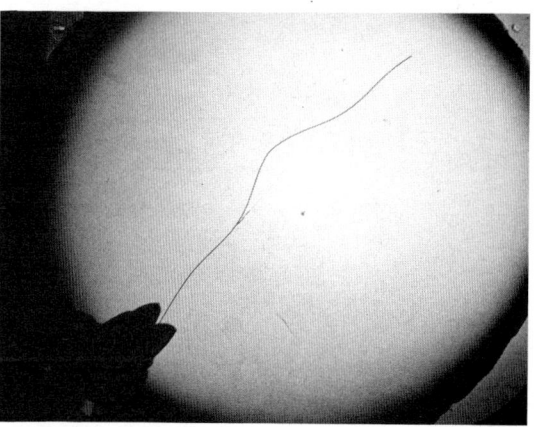

Program Outline

SOLIDS, LIQUIDS, AND GASES

1. **Chemists Experiment**
    A. What Do Chemists Do?
    B. Giant Test-Tube Experiment

2. **Define Matter/Energy: Quiz**

3. **Classify Solids, Liquids, and Gases**
    A. Classification Game
    B. Slides

4. **Investigate Phase Changes**
    A. Strawberry Gas: Fast Evaporators
    B. Dry Ice: Sublimation
    C. Iodine Gas: Sublimation
    D. On Other Planets

5. **Introduce the Concept of Atoms**
    A. What Is Matter Made Of?
    B. How Many Atoms Are in My Body?
    C. Atoms Are Always Moving

6. **Model Arrangements of Atoms in Solids, Liquids, and Gases**
    A. Dot Model/BB Model
    B. People Model

7. **Applying the Concepts**
    A. Balloon in Liquid Nitrogen
    B. Parsley in Liquid Nitrogen
    C. Nitinol Wire

8. **Conclusion**

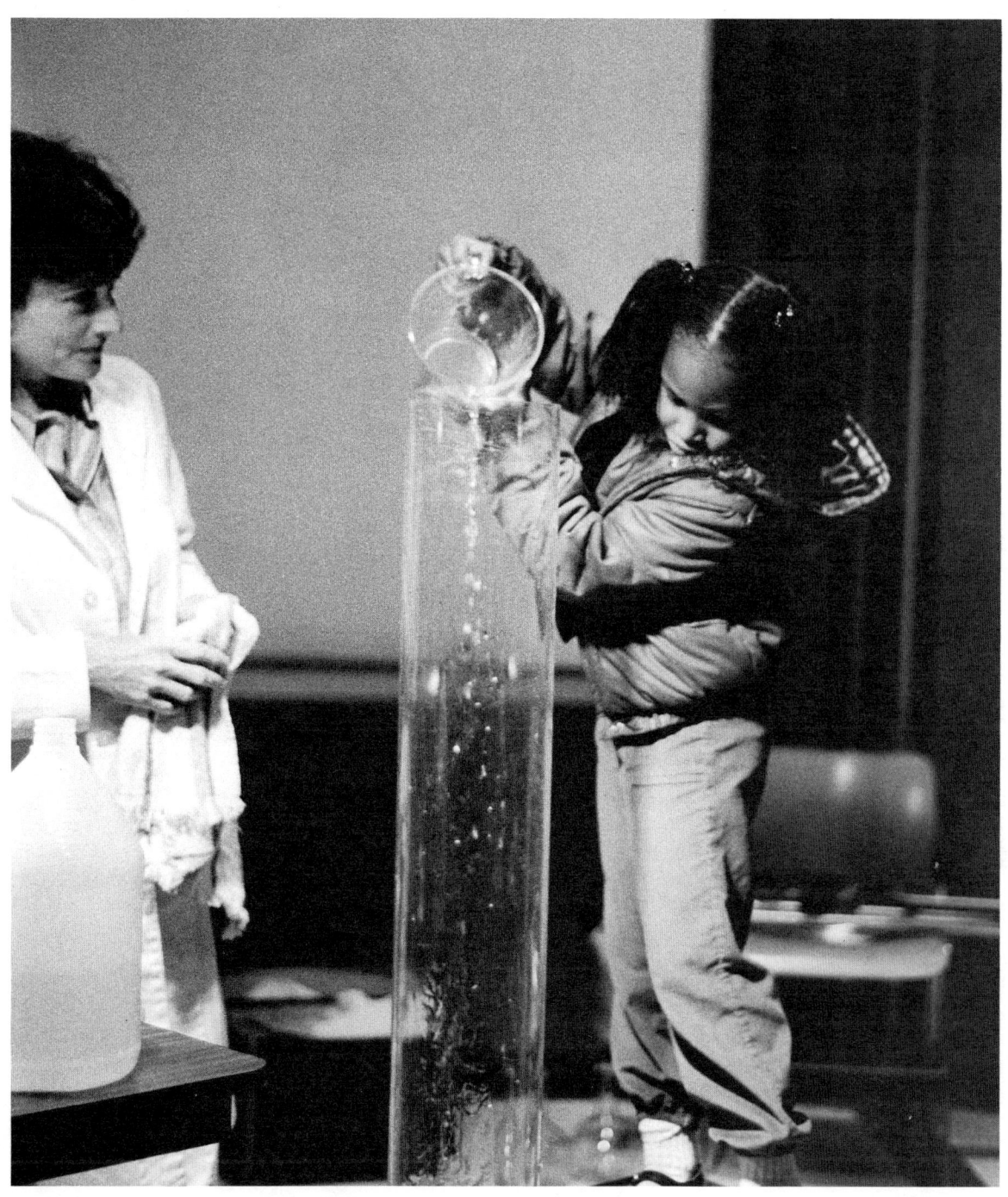

Program Outline 23

Presenting the Assembly Program

BEFORE THE ASSEMBLY

Learning the Program: Learning to present the program may seem like an enormous task. However, the sequence of demonstrations, experiments, and slides ensures a smooth flowing performance, without the necessity of memorizing a script. For the first few presentations, you may wish to use the one-page outline as a prompter to create your own cue cards.

Site Requirements: School auditoriums are the most common presentation sites, but it's also possible that you will find yourself presenting in school cafeterias, community centers, classrooms, and maybe even outdoors. The site must have electrical outlets and two long tables. Water must be convenient, and a screen available. For full effect you should be able to darken the room, and it's nice if there is a person to operate the lights on cue from you.

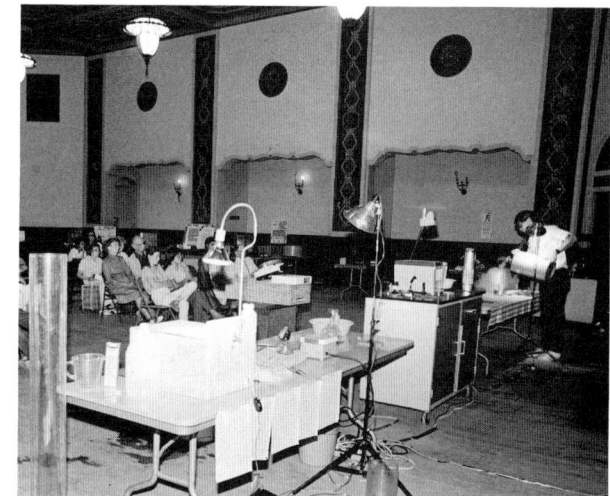

Transporting Materials: You may decide to present *Solids, Liquids, and Gases* at different sites. Most of the materials for the program pack neatly into five medium-sized boxes, and can be transported in a station wagon or a van. Several items, such as the liquid nitrogen Dewar, won't fit in boxes and so should be secured during transit with strong elastic cords or ropes. A long, cardboard box should be constructed to house the giant acrylic test tube during transit. A small, easily portable hand truck or wheeled-cart makes transport of materials from vehicle to presentation site much easier and more efficient. (See page 49 for a "Checklist of Materials" to bring with you.)

Setting Up Equipment: Plan on one hour for setup. The first step is to locate the projection screen and set up the slide projector to create an image as high as possible. Set the projector on a low cart or table so it will not obstruct the view; or use a long-throw lens and place the projector behind the audience.

Then set up two large tables in front of the screen. Place the overhead projector on one of the tables, and the hot plate and light box on the other table. Set up the light on its light stand in the center, behind both tables. Plug the equipment into a power strip. At the far end of the overhead projector table *(farthest from the hot plate)*, set up the equipment for the liquid nitrogen demonstrations. Place the giant test-tube and the step-stool at the end of the other table.

Place all small equipment on the tables, near where each item will be used. (Refer to page 54, "Setting Up at the Site" for a diagram outlining a suggested equipment arrangement.) Remember that if you have to search for something longer than 10–15 seconds, you will lose your audience's attention. Packing equipment in boxes according to the table the equipment will be on enables the presenter to quickly unpack the materials and set them in their proper places.

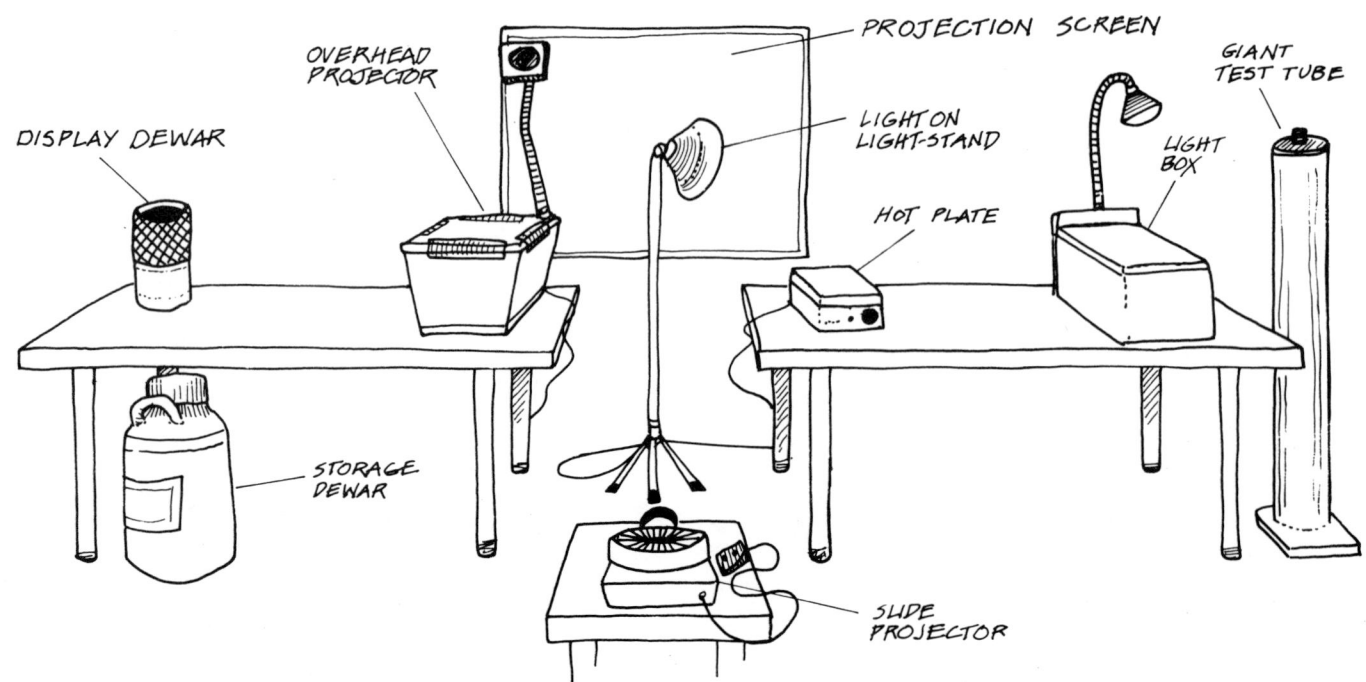

26 *Presenting the Assembly Program*

Refer to page 56 for a "Checklist of Last-Minute Tasks" to do at the site before presenting the assembly.

Audience Arrangements: Arrange seating so that the audience has a clear view of the demonstration area.

Costumes: Elementary school students enjoy the portrayal of "The Scientist" wearing a white lab coat. Putting on the white coat also gives the presenter an opportunity to introduce a few words on safety.

DURING THE ASSEMBLY

Questions: Here's how you can get into trouble. Imagine asking a group of 300 elementary school students: "What color do you see? Bedlam ensues as each student tries to make her "Violet!" heard over a chorus of "Red!" "Purple!" and "Blue!" The problem with asking an open-ended question in a large group context is that everyone wants to be heard. One way to deal with this is to ask the students to raise their hands, and allow time for several individuals to respond, one at a time. Another effective method is to eliminate a question altogether, and instead poll the audience to get their input: "Raise your hand if you see violet." Always let the students know in what way you want them to answer a question.

Responses: Whenever possible, think of ways to allow your audience to respond with hand signals. For example: "Hold up one finger if you think this is solid; two fingers if you think it's a liquid; and three fingers if you think it's a gas." This allows each individual in your audience to respond quickly and quietly.

Accepting Answers: What do you do when students give incorrect answers? Simply saying "that's wrong" will make the student feel bad and inhibit further responses to your questions. If you can, find something right about the responses. Let the student know that his answer was a logical one, but that there may be a better answer. For example, when asked why a frozen balloon shrinks, a student might say "Because atoms shrink when they get cold." You might respond with: "If atoms could shrink, that could explain why the balloon got smaller; but atoms always stay the same size. Does anybody have a different idea?" Another good technique is to listen to several answers without judgment. Don't stop when you get the right answer. When you've collected several answers, say "Those are all good ideas. A chemist would answer the question this way..."

Quiet Signs: Assembly program demonstrations are very exciting; it will be important to be able to get everyone's attention after one of the more spectacular displays. It is best to let the students know at the beginning of the program that a certain sign will mean "Quiet please, all eyes forward."

Microphone Techniques: Sixty minutes is a long time for elementary students to sit still. Variety in the presentation will help hold their attention. Vary your tone of voice and volume. One technique that is effective is to whisper into the microphone, so the students sense the drama and importance of what you're saying.

Styles: Many different styles of presentation are effective. Some presenters prefer to be dramatic, playing the role of "The Scientist" to the hilt. Others prefer a more intimate style, confiding secrets of science to the audience. Have fun developing your own unique style.

Younger Audiences: With K–2 students, focus more on classification and properties of matter and less on the more difficult concepts presented in the program. Leave out the finer distinctions and exceptions to rules: present glass as a solid and milk as a liquid, shorten the section on atoms and how they're arranged in solids, liquids, and gases. Simplify.

Older Audiences: While we do not recommend a fundamental change in the content of the program for junior high, high school, and adult audiences, it is important to orient the presentation to a higher level. Spend less time demonstrating the simple classification scheme of matter. Instead, you may point out some of the limits of classification systems. Mention substances that are difficult to classify such as liquid crystals, colloids, and plasmas. Offer more information. When talking about phase change and temperature, consider examples of materials at extreme temperatures such as molten lava, a meteor falling into the earth's atmosphere, or the temperature of the sun. Talk about the uses of liquid nitrogen and nitinol. Allow more time for questions from the audience.

AFTER THE ASSEMBLY

Packing Up: Allow about one half hour to break the equipment down and pack it up. Remember, the more care you put into storing the materials, the easier your preparation for the next show will be.

Demonstrations and Materials

The most important factor to consider when assembling materials for use in demonstrations is visibility: making sure that people in the back of the group can see. One technique is to use big things: four-foot test tubes, large flasks (one-liter capacity or more), etc. Another approach is to project images of materials on a projection screen, using an overhead projector or a slide projector. You can also highlight objects by darkening the room and then holding an object under a spotlight. This section includes a description of each of the demonstrations presented in *Solids, Liquids, and Gases*. At the end of this section you will find descriptions of the equipment used to enhance the visibility of the demonstrations: the light box, the spotlight, the overhead projector, and the slide projector.

1. GIANT TEST-TUBE EXPERIMENT

Materials

- [ ] 1 clear, pyrex, one-quart measuring cup
- [ ] 1 clear, one-cup measure
- [ ] 1 quart of vinegar
- [ ] 1 pound of baking soda
- [ ] 1 four-foot-long, 6" diameter, clear acrylic cylinder mounted on a base (8" x 8" x ½")
- [ ] 1 cylinder lid with balloon attachment nipple
- [ ] 1 small cork to stopper hole in cylinder lid
- [ ] 1 or 2 very large balloons (2 ft. diameter)
- [ ] 1 step-stool
- [ ] 1 light box

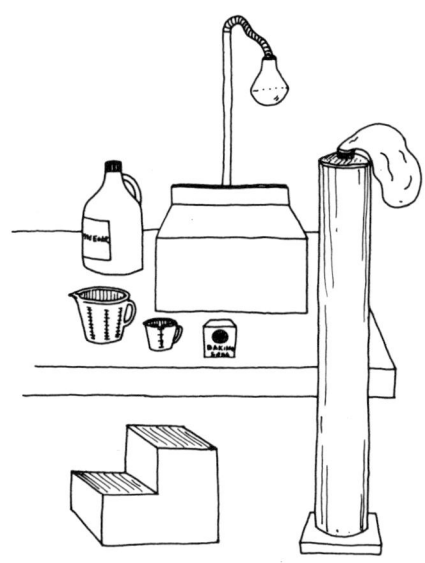

Construction of the Four-Foot Acrylic Cylinder

- [ ] 1 four-foot-long, 6" diameter, clear acrylic cylinder (⅛- to ½-inch wall thickness)
- [ ] 1 eight-inch square piece of ½-inch acrylic
- [ ] acrylic solvent cement
- [ ] 1 metal lathe

Using a metal lathe, mill a six-inch-wide, ¼-inch-deep, circular groove in the square piece of acrylic plastic. Use acrylic solvent cement to attach the cylinder to this base.

Construction of the Cylinder Lid with Valve

- [ ] 1 seven-inch-square piece of ½-inch acrylic
- [ ] 1 ¼-inch tapered pipe thread tap
- [ ] 1 ¼-inch threaded nipple, 1½"–2" long
- [ ] 1 large one-holed rubber stopper (to fit over the nipple, large enough so the neck of the balloon will stretch over it, allowing no gas to escape)
- [ ] 1 rubber O-ring (to fit the groove in the lid)

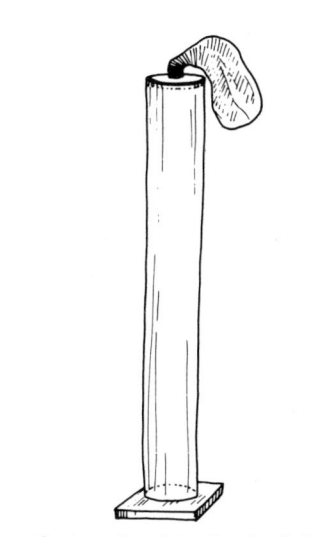

GIANT TEST TUBE

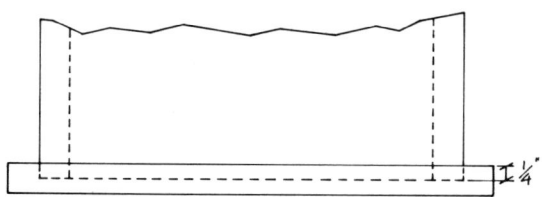

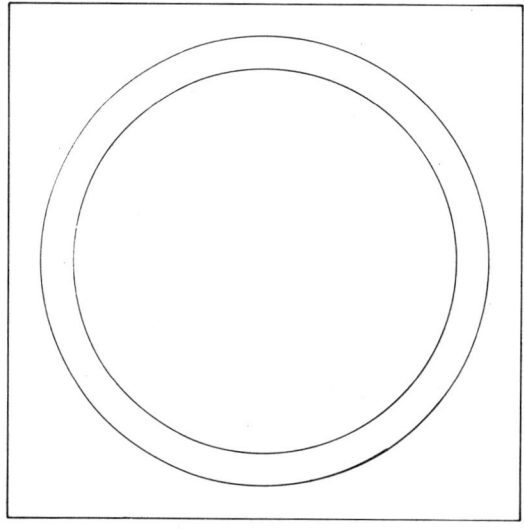

CYLINDER BASE

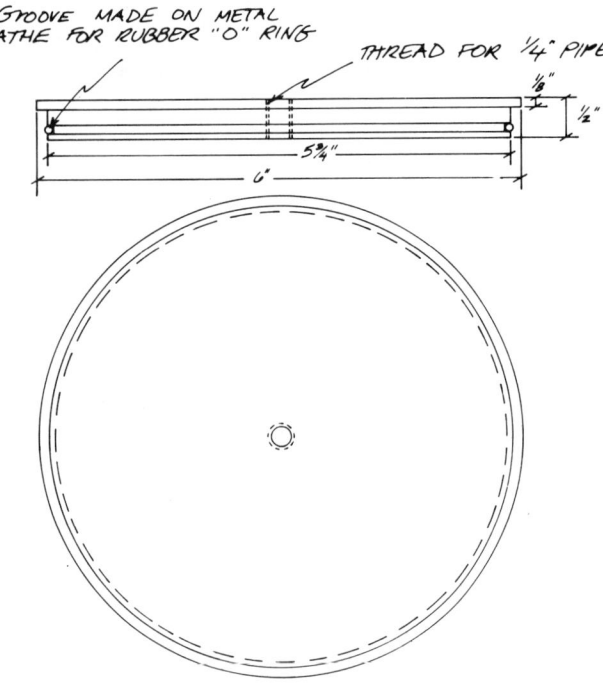

CYLINDER LID

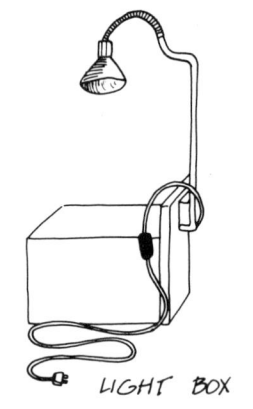

LIGHT BOX

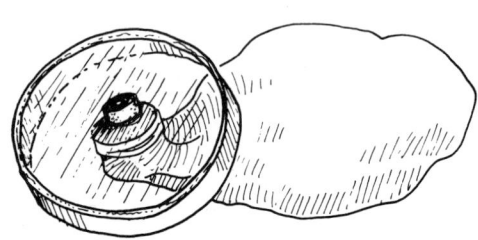

BALLOON ON LID

Use a metal lathe to turn a lid to fit the top of the acrylic cylinder, including the lip and groove for an O-ring. (See diagram.) Drill and tap a central hole for a ¼″ pipe nipple, 2″ long. Bore a rubber stopper with a large hole and run it onto the nipple, small taper end first.

Construction of the Light Box

See description and illustration on page 44.

Before the Program

Set the giant tube and the step-stool at the end of the table next to the light. Stretch the end of the balloon so it fits over the rubber stopper on the end of the top of the cylinder lid. Place the lid and all of the remaining materials on the table next to the light box.

During the Program

Put the one-quart measuring cup on the light box and fill the cup with vinegar. Have a volunteer climb the step-stool and pour vinegar into the giant tube. Pour one cup of baking soda into the small measuring cup on the light box. Instruct a second volunteer to dump the baking soda, all at once, into the tube, and quickly move the cup away. Immediately place the cylinder lid on the tube, using both hands, as the pressure from the gas will be great. The balloon attached to the rubber stopper on the lid will inflate. Keep holding the lid down as you talk. When you are ready to remove the lid, stopper the hole in the bottom of the lid with a small cork. You will lose a small amount of gas. Set aside the inflated balloon still attached to the lid for use in a later demonstration.

Background

Baking soda and vinegar react to form carbon dioxide gas.

2. MATTER/ENERGY QUIZ

Materials

- ☐ 1 medium-sized balloon
- ☐ 2 sheets of flash paper (about 3" x 5"
  —available at magic shops)
- ☐ 1 hot plate
- ☐ 1 light box

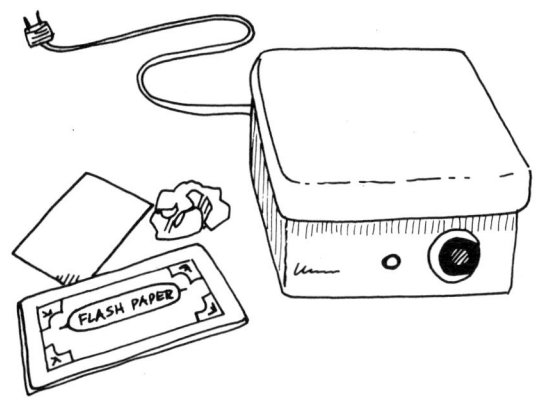

Before the Program

Turn on the hot plate and leave it on throughout the show. Crumple the pieces of flash paper and put them in the pocket of your lab coat.

During the Program

When you are ready to ignite the flash paper, slip it into your hand and bring your hand close to the surface of the hot plate. This will ignite the flash paper. As the paper catches fire, quickly lift your hand into the air, so the audience will see a "trail of fire."

Background

Flash paper is coated with a highly combustible chemical. When the combustion point of this chemical is reached, the paper will burst into flames. The combustion occurs so quickly that your hand will not have time to get hot.

Demonstrations and Materials 33

3. CLASSIFICATION GAME

Materials

- ☐ 1 "SOLID" sign
- ☐ 1 "LIQUID" sign
- ☐ 1 "GAS" sign
- ☐ 1 rock
- ☐ 1 inflated balloon (from demonstration 1)
- ☐ 1 one-liter glass flask half-full of water
- ☐ 1 flower, piece of fruit, or vegetable

Making the SOLID, LIQUID, GAS signs

- ☐ about 6 ft. of medium-weight string
- ☐ 3 pieces of 8½" x 11" poster board, each a different color
- ☐ white paper for letters
- ☐ rubber cement
- ☐ 1 one-hole paper punch
- ☐ laminating film or clear contact paper
- ☐ scissors

Make three signs: the first should have a large "SOLID" written on one side, and a giant "S" on the other. The second should have "LIQUID" and "L" back-to-back. Do the same for "GAS" and "G." Laminate, punch, and string up your signs. In small rooms, volunteers should display words; in large rooms, the letters can be seen more easily.

4. STRAWBERRY GAS

Materials

- [ ] 1 bottle of strawberry extract (coconut flavor works well, too)
- [ ] 1 glass Petri dish (4" diameter)
- [ ] 1 overhead projector
- [ ] 1 hot plate
- [ ] 1 hot-pad holder
- [ ] 1 piece of wire screen (about 5" square to place hot Petri dish on)
- [ ] 1 bucket of sand or a fire extinguisher

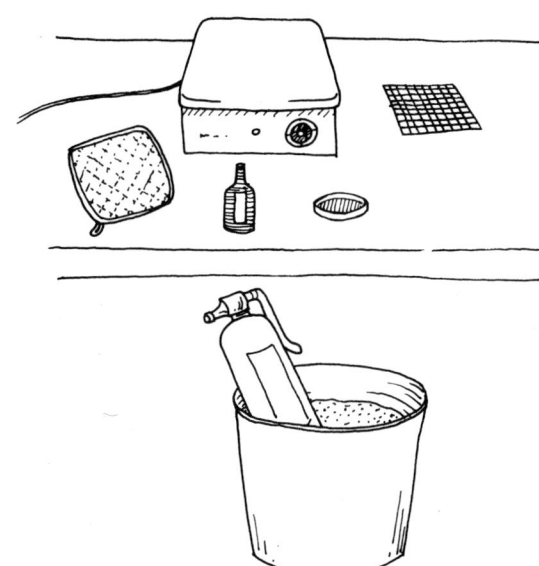

Before the Program

Put the bucket of sand or a fire extinguisher under the table, near the hot plate. Place the hot-pad holder and the wire screen on the table next to the hot plate. Put the rest of the materials on the other table, next to the overhead projector.

During the Program

Turn the overhead projector on. Pour the strawberry extract into the glass Petri dish on the projector, so the red liquid is projected on the screen. Put the Petri dish on the hot plate. When most of the liquid has evaporated, use the hot-pad holder to remove the hot Petri dish from the hot plate and place it on the wire screen.

5. DRY ICE

Materials

- [ ] dry ice (4" x 8" slab is plenty)
- [ ] 1 styrofoam dry-ice keeper
- [ ] 1 clear glass container large enough to place the piece of dry ice in
- [ ] 1 screwdriver
- [ ] 1 pair of leather gloves
- [ ] 1 light box
- [ ] about 1 quart of hot water
- [ ] 1 kettle (to heat water in)
- [ ] several drops of food coloring to color water
- [ ] 1 hot plate
- [ ] 1 piece of wire screen (about 5 inches square) to place hot kettle on

Before the Program

Heat water in the kettle on the hot plate. Place the hot kettle on the screen under the table near the light box. Water should still be warm when you're ready to use it, about 30 minutes into the program. Put three or four drops of food coloring in the clear glass container. Place the container under the table near the light box. Put the dry ice keeper (containing the dry ice) and the leather gloves on the floor near the light box table. Use the screwdriver to break off a piece of dry ice that will fit in your glass container.

During the Program

Put on the leather gloves and take a piece of dry ice out of the dry ice keeper. Hit the ice on the surface of the light box so the audience can hear that dry ice is a solid. Hold the dry ice under the warm light so the audience can see the dry ice sublime. Pour warm water into the clear container. Put the dry ice in the water. After 30 seconds or so, blow across the top of the container, causing the "fog" to billow.

6. IODINE GAS

Materials

- [ ] iodine crystals
- [ ] 1 small plastic Petri dish
- [ ] 1 test tube with cork
- [ ] 1 overhead projector
- [ ] 1 large Florence flask
- [ ] 1 rubber stopper that fits neck of flask
- [ ] 1 hot plate
- [ ] 1 piece of wire screen (about 5 inches square) to put under hot flask
- [ ] 1 light box

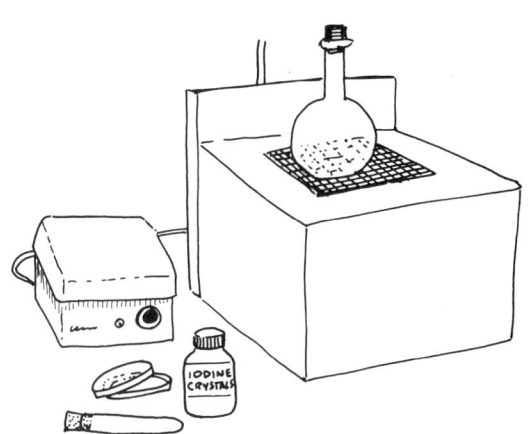

Before the Program

Shake 4–6 iodine crystals into a test tube and cork it. The iodine crystals will sublime very slowly, even when in the test tube. Place this test tube and an empty Petri dish near the overhead projector. Put the wire screen and the rubber stopper near the light box. Put the Florence flask near the hot plate.

During the Program

At the beginning of the iodine demonstration, place the flask on the hot plate to heat up. Turn on the overhead projector. Transfer the iodine crystals to the Petri dish, then set this dish on the overhead projector. Remove the heated flask from the hot plate, and set the flask on the screen, on top of the light box. *Drop the crystals into the flask and stop it up so no gas escapes. Iodine gas is toxic.*

Background

Heat causes the iodine crystals to sublime (turn directly to gas), producing violet-colored iodine gas. As the flask cools, the iodine will recrystallize all over the inside surfaces of the flask, especially in the neck of the flask. When you can no longer observe the violet-colored gas, you can remove the stopper and rinse the flask out with water or alcohol (alcohol is more effective).

7. HOW MANY ATOMS ARE IN MY BODY?

Materials

☐ 1 standard yellow pencil with eraser

Background

The radius of a hydrogen atom is 10^{-8} cm.

8. ATOMS ARE ALWAYS MOVING

Materials

☐ 1 fiber optics "wand" (commercially available)

During the Program

Turn out the lights. Turn on the fiber optics wand, and wiggle it quickly and constantly, causing the strands of the fiber optics to fly around the lighted center of the wand.

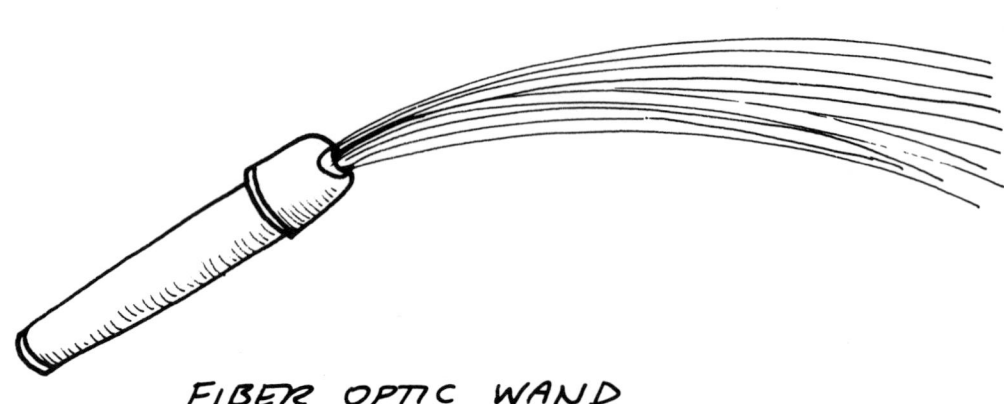

FIBER OPTIC WAND

9. DOT MODEL/BB MODEL

Materials

- ☐ 1 overhead projector
- ☐ 1 atoms-in-a-solid overlay
- ☐ 1 atoms-in-a-liquid overlay
- ☐ 1 atoms-in-a-gas overlay
- ☐ 1 solid BB model
- ☐ 1 liquid BB model
- ☐ 1 gas BB model

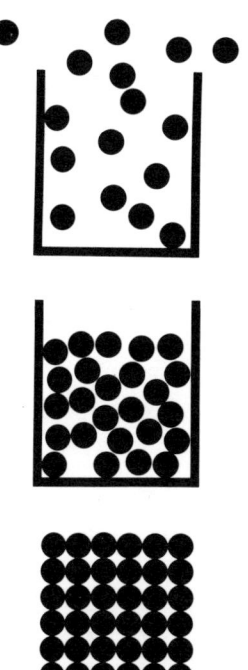

Construction of Dot Models

- ☐ 1 colored marker made for writing on plastic
- ☐ 3 8½" x 11" sheets of plastic for making overlays

Construction of BB Models

- ☐ 3 plastic Petri dishes (about 4" in diameter)
- ☐ a handful of BBs
- ☐ glue

Put BBs in Petri dishes. Glue tops of dishes to bottoms of dishes so the BBs will not fly out when the dishes are shaken.

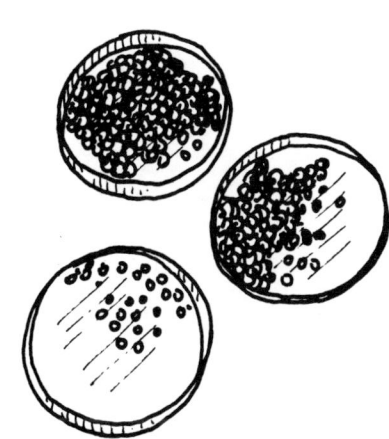

During the Program

Turn on the overhead projector. Alternately project the dot model overlay and the BB model for each phase: solid, liquid, and gas. To model a solid using the BB model, move the Petri dish back and forth slowly so the BBs vibrate. To model a liquid, move the dish of BBs faster so the BBs appear to move "fluidly." To model a gas, move the dish of BBs back and forth rapidly, so the BBs appear as a blur. Repeat the demonstration, however this time model the changes of solid→liquid→gas→liquid→solid using only the BB models.

10. and 11. BALLOON AND PARSLEY IN LIQUID NITROGEN

Materials

- ☐ 1–2 liters liquid nitrogen
- ☐ 1 storage Dewar (special triple vacuum-sealed container for holding extremely cold liquids)
- ☐ 1 wide-mouth display Dewar (1 liter capacity)
- ☐ 1 pair of safety goggles
- ☐ 1 pair of metal tongs
- ☐ 1 pair of leather gloves
- ☐ 2 inflated balloons (long and thin, to fit into display Dewar)
- ☐ 1 bunch of parsley (or carrot tops or other leafy bouquet)
- ☐ 1 spotlight mounted on light stand
- ☐ 1 tablecloth

Before the Program

Inflate two balloons. Spread the tablecloth on the overhead projector table. (The tablecloth will keep the liquid nitrogen from "bouncing" off the hard surface of the table.) Place the display Dewar and all other materials on the portion of the table covered with the tablecloth. Put on the gloves and a pair of safety goggles, and "prime" the display Dewar by pouring a small amount of liquid nitrogen into it. This will allow the container to cool down more gradually. Store the storage Dewar under the overhead projector table.

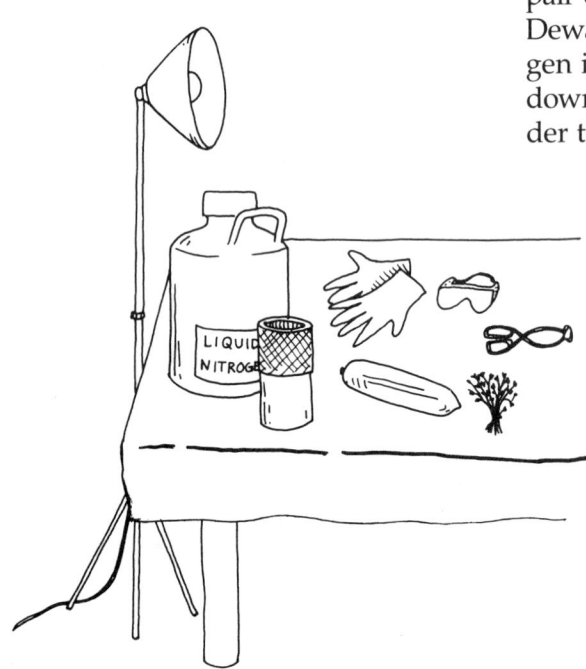

40 Demonstrations and Materials

During the Program

Turn off the house lights, and turn on the spotlight. Put on the safety goggles and leather gloves, and pour liquid nitrogen from the large Dewar until it fills the smaller Dewar. Hold up an inflated balloon. With the pair of tongs, submerge the balloon in the liquid nitrogen. Wait about 5–10 seconds until the nitrogen almost stops boiling. Remove the balloon from the liquid nitrogen and hold it under the spotlight; this works best if you heat it evenly with a back-and-forth, rotating motion. The second balloon is a backup in case the first one pops.

Hold up a bunch of parsley. Using the tongs, lower the parsley into the liquid nitrogen. Leave it in until the liquid nitrogen almost stops boiling. Remove the parsley from the nitrogen and hold the parsley under the light. Crush the parsley with your other gloved hand.

A banana or a rubber ball may also be frozen and then shattered. However, you must allow close to five minutes for these thicker items to freeze. Parsley will freeze in less than a minute.

Background

The temperature of liquid nitrogen is $-320°$ F. Objects left in the nitrogen until it stops boiling will become the temperature of the liquid nitrogen. This will cause some gases to liquefy, most liquids to change to solids, and most solids to become very brittle. Taking energy away from atoms (by cooling them) causes the atoms to slow down and move closer together. When placed in the liquid nitrogen, the balloon will shrink. Some of the gases inside the balloon may change to liquid (oxygen, carbon dioxide). The parsley will shatter, making the sound of glass shattering.

12. NITINOL WIRE

Nitinol wire may be ordered from:

Flinn Scientific
P.O. Box 219
Batavia, Illinois 60510
1-800-452-1261

Note: Flinn Scientific sells nitinol wire *only* to teachers.

Materials

- [ ] 1 six-inch piece of nitinol wire (0.0060 > 0.0048 gauge)
- [ ] 1 pencil
- [ ] 1 clock crystal with a flat face (the glass cover of a wall clock)
- [ ] 1 overhead projector
- [ ] about two cups of warm water
- [ ] about two cups of ice water
- [ ] 2 insulated bottles
- [ ] 1 plastic dishpan

Before the Program

Get some warm water (from a tap or from the kettle of warm water used in Demonstration 5) and store it in one insulated bottle. Store ice water in the second insulated bottle. Place all of the materials on the table near the overhead projector.

During the Program

Turn on the overhead projector. Turn off the house lights. Project a piece of nitinol wire on the screen. Pull back on the top of the wire and then release it so the audience can see the wire spring back. Pour ice water from the insulated bottle into the plastic dishpan. Submerge the wire and then wrap it around a pencil. Hold the wire on the overhead projector so the wire's corkscrew shape is projected on the screen. Now put the clock crystal on the overhead projector. Fill the crystal with warm water from the other insulated bottle. Hold the wire just over the surface of the water so the wire's image is projected on the wall, but the wire is not touching the water. Lower the wire into the water, a little at a time. The nitinol wire will suddenly straighten.

Background

Nitinol is a nickel-titanium alloy. When its temperature goes from cold to hot, nitinol undergoes a very subtle phase change, from one solid-state phase to another. The temperature change causes the atoms in nitinol's crystal lattice to change position. This phase change is accompanied by an abrupt change in the properties of nitinol and by sudden movement. Though the mechanism by which heat energy is converted to mechanical energy is not completely understood, scientists are working to employ nitinol's unique properties in building various kinds of "heat engines."

13. LIGHT BOX

Construction

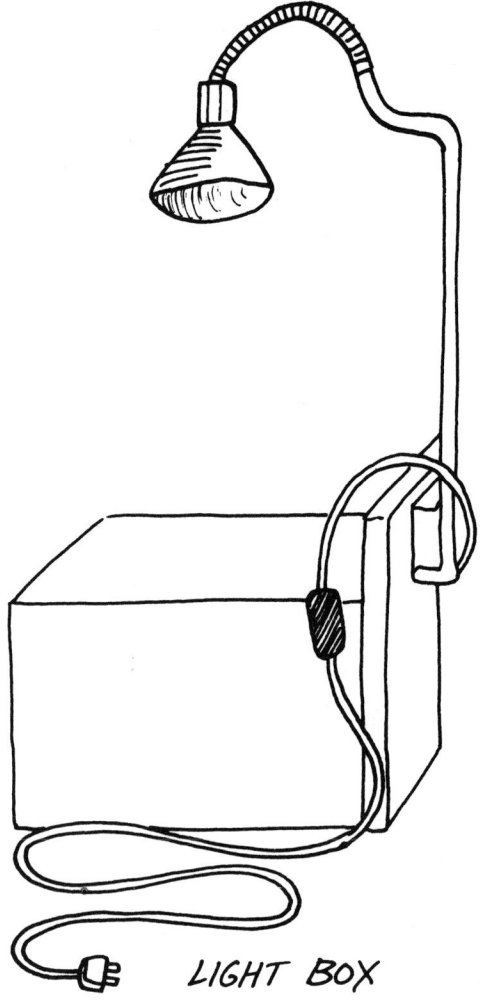

LIGHT BOX

- ☐ 1 wooden box (with a surface of at least 12" x 12" and a height of about 8 inches)
- ☐ 1 spotlight
- ☐ 1 flexible lamp arm
- ☐ materials for mounting light to box
- ☐ electrical cord
- ☐ switch
- ☐ plug

A light box provides a flat, elevated surface on which to perform demonstrations, illuminated by a spotlight. The spotlight is best mounted on some sort of a flexible arm that will allow you to point the light in a variety of directions. There should be an on-off switch mounted either on the cord or on the light itself. The method of construction you select will depend on what materials are available to you. This diagram shows one way to construct a light box.

Before the Program

Place the light box at the far end of the hot plate table, and plug it into the power strip.

During the Program

Conduct demonstrations on the platform of the light box. Change the position of the spotlight, and turn the light on and off as needed. Use a square of metal screen to protect the wooden surface of the box when using hot objects.

14. SPOTLIGHT ON A LIGHT STAND

Construction

- ☐ 1 spotlight
- ☐ 1 light stand (like those used by photographers)

Before the Program

Set the spotlight on the lightstand in the center, behind both tables.

During the Program

Turn the spotlight on and off, and change the position of the spotlight as needed.

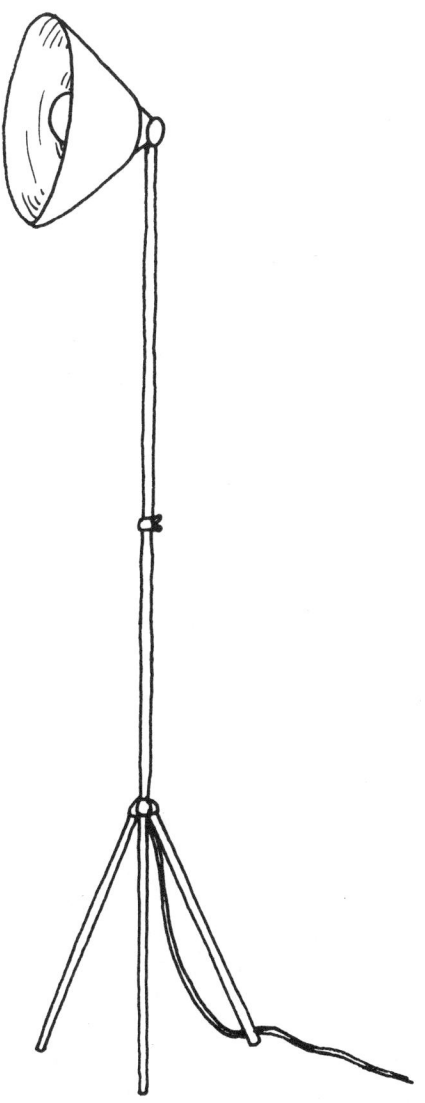

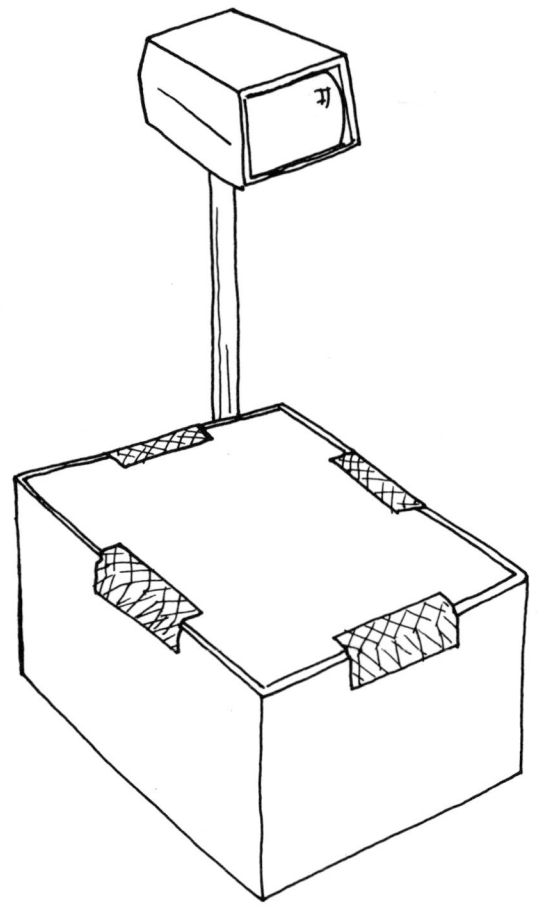

15. OVERHEAD PROJECTOR

Construction

- [ ] 1 overhead projector
- [ ] 1 rectangular piece of clear acrylic plastic, large enough to cover the platform of the overhead projector
- [ ] duct tape
- [ ] 1 projection screen

Tape the acrylic plastic so it covers the surface of the overhead projector. This will protect the inside of the projector from the inevitable spills that occur.

Before the Program

Place the overhead projector on the table so the image can be projected on the screen.

During the Program

Use the overhead projector to project transparent or silhouette images.

16. SLIDE PROJECTOR AND SLIDES

Materials

- ☐ 10 slides
- ☐ 1 slide projector with remote control
- ☐ 1 projection screen
- ☐ 1 slide selector extension

Slides are shown at various points throughout the program both for enhancement and to capitalize on the variety that is provided by a multi-media presentation. The slides suggested are ones that work well, however they are not absolutely necessary. Create your own slide sequence, duplicate ours, or leave out slides altogether. See page 55 for a list of slides and current ordering information.

Before the Program

Set up the slide projector as described in *"Setting Up Equipment"* on p. 26. Run the remote controller to the edge of the overhead projector table, using the slide selector extension cord if necessary. Use duct tape to tape these cords to the floor. Turn on the slide projector and focus the first slide on the screen.

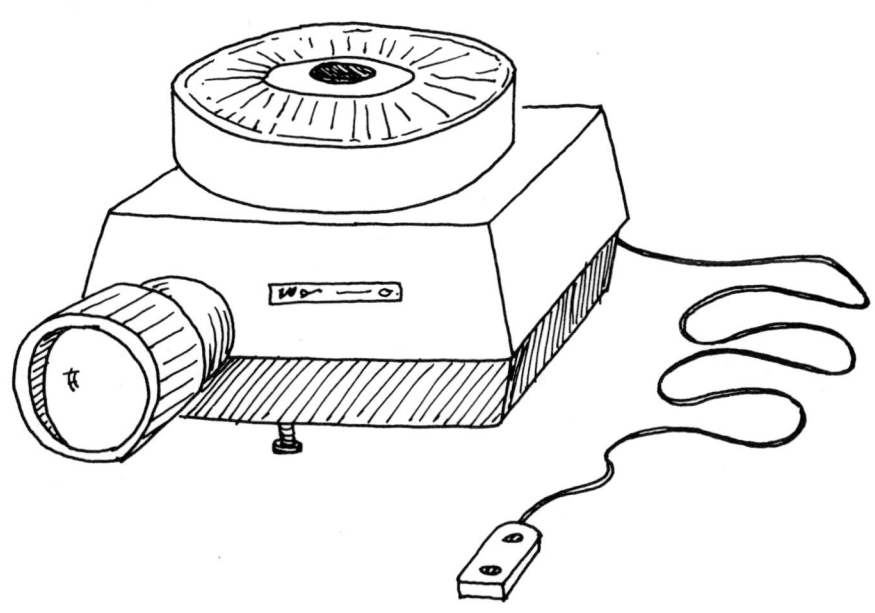

Demonstrations and Materials

17. POWER STRIP AND EXTENSION CORDS

Materials

☐ 1 power strip
☐ 1 50-foot extension cord
☐ 2 15-foot extension cords
☐ 1 roll of duct tape

Before the Program

Be sure to use duct tape to tape all cords to the floor so neither you nor the student volunteers will trip over these cords during the assembly.

18. MICROPHONE

Before the Program

Most auditoriums are equipped with microphones. Find out if one will be available. You may wish to bring a microphone and amplifier with you. If you have a strong voice that projects well, you may not need a microphone; but you should arrange for people to observe how well your voice carries in a full auditorium.

If you are using the school public address system, get the school custodian to set it up and be sure to test it before the students arrive.

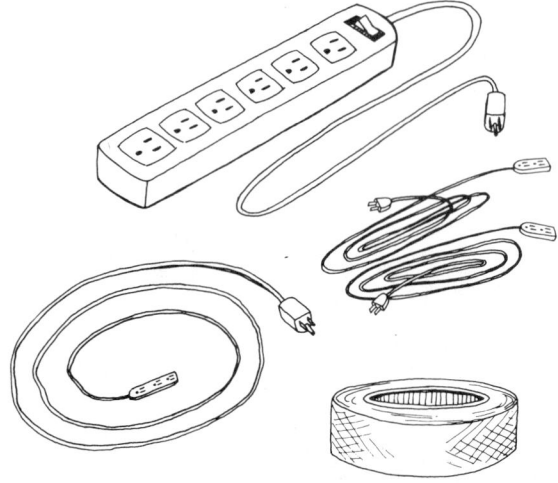

Checklist of Materials

1. Giant Test-Tube Experiment

- ☐ 1 clear, pyrex, one-quart measuring cup
- ☐ 1 clear, one-cup measuring cup
- ☐ 1 quart of vinegar
- ☐ 1 lb. of baking soda
- ☐ 1 four-foot, clear acrylic cylinder mounted on a base
- ☐ 1 cylinder lid with nipple
- ☐ 1 small cork to stopper hole in cylinder lid
- ☐ 1 or 2 very large balloons (2 ft. diameter)
- ☐ 1 step-stool
- ☐ 1 light box

2. Matter/Energy Quiz

- ☐ 1 medium-sized balloon
- ☐ 2 sheets of flash paper (about 3" x 5")
- ☐ 1 hot plate
- ☐ 1 light box

3. Classification Game

- ☐ 1 "SOLID" sign
- ☐ 1 "LIQUID" sign
- ☐ 1 "GAS" sign
- ☐ 1 rock
- ☐ 1 inflated balloon (from demonstration 1)
- ☐ 1 one-liter glass flask half-full of water
- ☐ 1 flower, piece of fruit, or vegetable

4. Strawberry Gas

- ☐ 1 bottle strawberry extract
- ☐ 1 glass Petri dish (4" in diameter)
- ☐ 1 overhead projector
- ☐ 1 hot plate
- ☐ 1 hot-pad holder
- ☐ 1 piece of wire screen (about 5" square)
- ☐ 1 bucket of sand or a fire extinguisher

5. Dry Ice

- ☐ dry ice (4" x 8" slab is plenty)
- ☐ 1 styrofoam dry ice keeper
- ☐ 1 clear glass container large enough to place the piece of dry ice in
- ☐ 1 screwdriver
- ☐ 1 pair of leather gloves
- ☐ 1 light box
- ☐ about 1 quart of hot water
- ☐ 1 kettle
- ☐ several drops of food coloring to color water
- ☐ 1 hot plate
- ☐ 1 piece of wire screen (about 5" square)

6. Iodine Gas

- ☐ iodine crystals
- ☐ 1 small plastic Petri dish
- ☐ 1 test tube with cork
- ☐ 1 overhead projector
- ☐ 1 large Florence flask
- ☐ 1 rubber stopper that fits neck of flask
- ☐ 1 hot plate
- ☐ 1 piece of wire screen (about 5" square)
- ☐ 1 light box

7. How Many Atoms Are in My Body?

- ☐ 1 standard yellow pencil with eraser

8. Atoms Are Always Moving

- ☐ 1 fiber optics "wand"

9. Dot Model/BB Model

- ☐ 1 overhead projector
- ☐ 1 atoms-in-a-solid overlay
- ☐ 1 atoms-in-a-liquid overlay
- ☐ 1 atoms-in-a-gas overlay
- ☐ 1 solid BB model
- ☐ 1 liquid BB model
- ☐ 1 gas BB model

10. and 11. Balloon and Parsley in Liquid Nitrogen

- ☐ 1–2 liters liquid nitrogen
- ☐ 1 storage Dewar
- ☐ 1 wide-mouth display Dewar (1 liter capacity)
- ☐ 1 pair of safety goggles
- ☐ 1 pair of metal tongs
- ☐ 1 pair of leather gloves
- ☐ 2 inflated balloons (long and thin, to fit into display Dewar)
- ☐ 1 bunch of parsley
- ☐ 1 spotlight mounted on light stand
- ☐ 1 tablecloth

12. Nitinol Wire

- ☐ 1 six-inch piece of nitinol wire
- ☐ 1 pencil
- ☐ 1 clock crystal with a flat face
- ☐ 1 overhead projector
- ☐ about two cups of warm water
- ☐ about two cups of ice water
- ☐ 2 insulated bottles
- ☐ 1 plastic dishpan

13. **Light Box**

14. **Spotlight on a Light Stand**

15. **Overhead Projector**

16. **Slide Projector and Slides**

    ☐ 10 slides
    ☐ 1 slide projector with remote control
    ☐ 1 projection screen
    ☐ 1 slide selector extension

17. **Power Strip and Extension Cords**

    ☐ 1 power strip
    ☐ 1 50-foot extension cord
    ☐ 2 15-foot extension cords
    ☐ roll of duct tape

18. **Microphone**

Setting Up at the Site

When you arrive at the presentation site, locate: two large tables for the equipment, one small table for the slide projector, a projection screen, electrical outlets, and a source of water.

Arranging the equipment in a logical order makes it much easier to present the program; you will be able to quickly scan the tables to find the equipment you want. Also, the materials themselves are very effective "cue cards," reminding you what comes next. We recommend the arrangement illustrated on the next page. The numbers correspond to the following key.

1. Leather gloves
2. Dry-ice keeper with dry ice
3. Screwdriver
4. Step-stool
5. Giant test tube
6. Cylinder lid with large balloon
7. Light box
8. Vinegar
9. One-quart measuring cup
10. One-cup measuring cup
11. Baking soda
12. Large glass jar
13. Tea kettle
14. Signs
15. Florence flask half full of water for classification game
16. Screen
17. Small balloon
18. Hot plate
19. Rubber stopper for iodine flask
20. Screen
21. Rock
22. Banana (for classification game)
23. Hot pad holder
24. Fire extinguisher
25. Sand bucket
26. 35 mm slide projector with remote control and slide selector extension
27. BB models
28. Overhead projector
29. Spotlight on stand
30. Nitinol wire and clock crystal
31. Pencil (for coiling nitinol wire)
32. Strawberry extract and glass Petri dish
33. Iodine crystals
34. Test tube with cork (for iodine crystals)

35. Plastic Petri dish
36. Pencil (for "How Many Atoms in My Body" demonstration)
37. Fiber optics wand
38. Florence flask (for iodine demonstration)
39. Plastic dishpan
40. Insulated bottle of hot water
41. Insulated bottle of cold water
42. Safety goggles
43. Tongs
44. Display Dewar
45. Parsley
46. 2 inflated balloons (for liquid nitrogen demonstration)
47. Dewar containing liquid nitrogen
48. White lab coat
49. Microphone

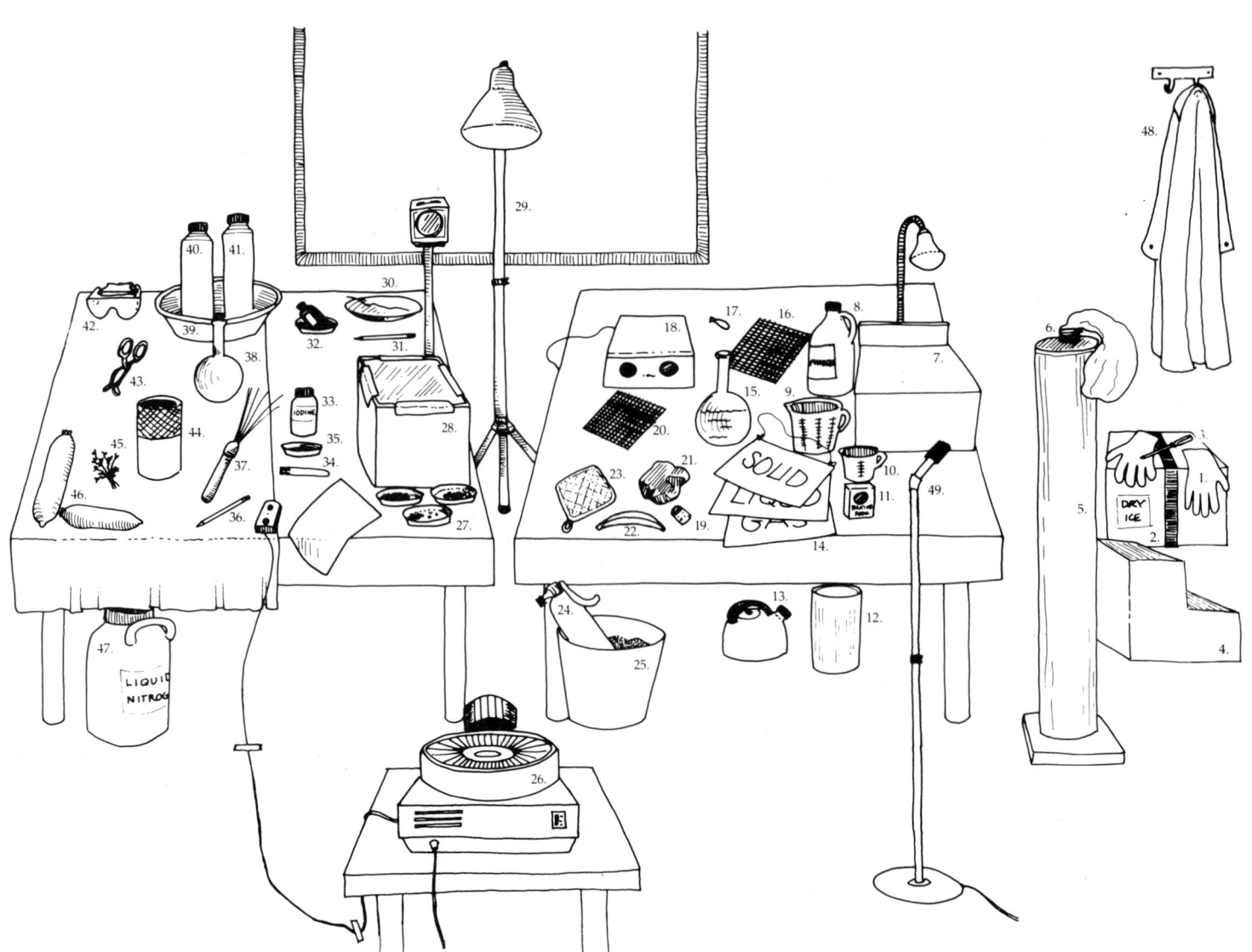

List of Slides

The following slides may be purchased by sending $26.50 (1999 price, does not include shipping) to:

GEMS SLIDES/SLG
Lawrence Hall of Science
University of California
Berkeley, CA 94720

Slide #1. Alchemist

Slide #2. Modern Day Chemist

Slide #3. Student Chemists

Slide #4. Hot Air Balloon

Slide #5. Old Glass Bottle

Slide #6. Ginger Ale

Slide #7. Milk

Slide #8. Phases of the elements at 60 degrees Fahrenheit

Slide #9. Phases of the elements at −346 degrees Fahrenheit

Slide #10. Phases of the elements at 788 degrees Fahrenheit

Checklist of Last-Minute Tasks

☐ Turn on hot plate.

☐ Heat a kettle full of water on the hot plate.

☐ Fill one insulated bottle with hot water (from a tap or from the kettle).

☐ Leave the remaining water in the kettle and place it under the light box table.

☐ Crumple two pieces of flash paper and place them in your pocket.

☐ Fill one Florence flask half full of water.

☐ Put several iodine crystals in a test tube and stopper it.

☐ Inflate two small balloons for the liquid nitrogen demonstration.

☐ Put 3–4 drops of food coloring in the clear glass container for the dry ice demonstration.

☐ Break off a small piece of dry ice.

☐ Turn on the slide projector and focus the first slide on the screen.

☐ If you are using the school public address system, get the school custodian to set it up and test it before the students arrive.

Literature Connections

A Chilling Story: How Things Cool Down
by Eve and Albert Stwertka; illustrated by Mena Dolobowsky
Julian Messner/Simon & Schuster, New York. 1991   *Grades: 4–8*
> How refrigeration and air conditioning work are explained simply, with sections on heat transfer, evaporation, and expansion. Humorous black and white drawings show a family and its cat testing out the principles in their home. This book connects well to the experiments involving dry ice and liquid nitrogen in the GEMS guide.

Everybody Needs a Rock
by Byrd Baylor; illustrated by Peter Parnall
Aladdin Books, New York. 1974   *Grades: K–5*
> This book describes the qualities to consider when selecting the perfect rock for play and pleasure. In so doing, the properties of color, size, shape, texture, and smell are discussed in such a way that you'll want to rush out and find a rock of your own. Nice introduction or follow-up to a discussion of the properties of solids.

Hot-Air Henry
by Mary Calhoun; illustrated by Erick Ingraham
William Morrow, New York. 1981   *Grades: K–3*
> Henry, a spunky Siamese cat, stows away on a hot air balloon and accidentally gets a solo flight. He learns that there is more to ballooning than just watching as he deals with air currents, power lines, and manipulating the gas burner. Though the format and style of the book are aimed at primary grades, information on ballooning and the more complex concept that hot air becomes less dense are also presented.

The Magic School Bus at the Waterworks
by Joanna Cole; illustrated by Bruce Degen
Scholastic, New York. 1986   *Grades: K–6*
> When Ms. Frizzle takes her class on a field trip to the waterworks, everyone ends up experiencing the water purification system from the inside. Evaporation, the water cycle, and filtration are just a few of the concepts explored in this whimsical field trip. The phase changes of water, from solid to liquid to gas, provide a familiar example for all ages of some of the concepts explored in this assembly presenter's guide.

Splash! All About Baths
by Susan K. Buxbaum and Rita G. Gelman;
illustrated by Maryann Cocca-Leffler
Little, Brown & Co., Boston. 1987   *Grades: K–6*
> Penguin answers his animal friends' questions about baths such as "What shape is water?" "Why do soap and water make you clean?" "What is a bubble?" "Why does the water go up when you get in?" "Why do some things float and others sink?" and other questions. Answers to questions are both clear and simple. Received the American Institute of Physics Science Writing Award.

Supersuits
by Vicki Cobb; illustrated by Peter Lippman
J.B. Lippincott, Philadelphia. 1975 *Grades: 4–7*

This book describes severe environmental conditions that require special clothing for survival such as freezing cold, fire, underwater work, and thin or non-existent air. "Going Where It's Cold" talks about solids, liquids, and gases at cold temperatures.

Very Last First Time
by Jan Andrews; illustrated by Ian Wallace
Atheneum, New York. 1986 *Grades: 2–4*

An Inuit girl, Eva, walks by herself (for the "very first last time") in a sea-floor cavern under the frozen ocean ice when the tide goes out, gathering mussels and making discoveries. Later, her candle goes out, and the tide starts to come roaring in, while the ice shrieks and creaks. Terrified at first, Eva recovers, and eventually finds her way to the surface and her waiting mother. Although the book does not scientifically explain the freezing of the top of the sea or the action of the tides, you and your class may want to discuss these questions: "Why does only the top part of the water freeze?" "Why does the ice stay intact even when the water underneath it goes out with the tide?" The images of Eva on the sea floor beneath the ice are unique and fascinating. The descriptive language and Eva's intense interest in nature exemplify excellent scientific observation skills.

Water's Way
by Lisa W. Peters; illustrated by Ted Rand
Arcade Publishing/Little, Brown & Co., New York. 1991 *Grades: K–3*

"Water has a way of changing" inside and outside Tony's house, from clouds to steam to fog and other forms. Illustrations show the changes in the weather outside while highlighting water changes inside the house.

For literature connections for all GEMS guides, we recommend the GEMS literature handbook, entitled *Once Upon A GEMS Guide: Connecting Young People's Literature to Great Explorations in Math and Science.*

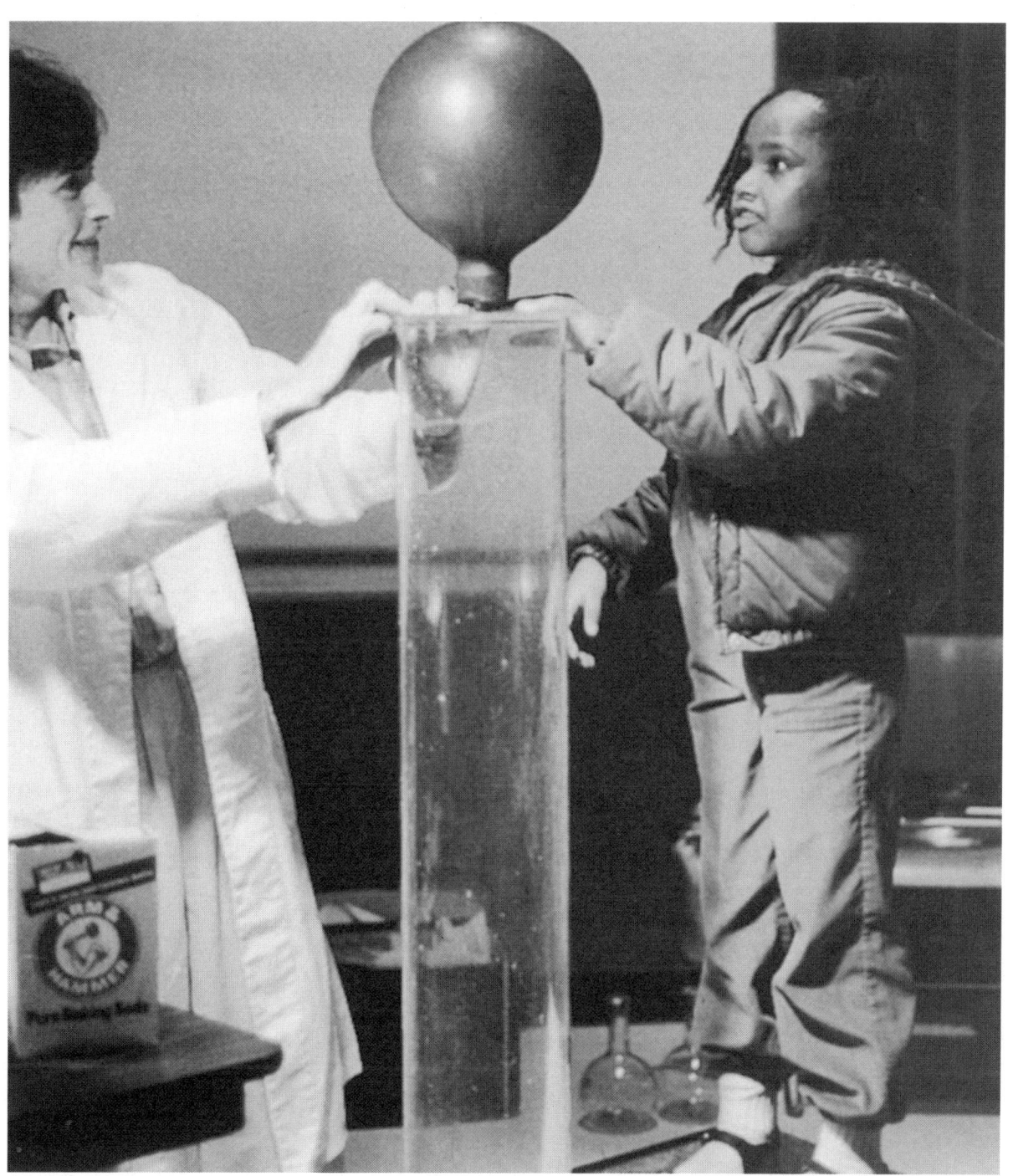

Notes